11-95

£6-

BOOKEND

SUNY Series, Postmodern Culture
Joseph Natoli, Editor

BOOKEND

Anatomies of a Virtual Self

Joe Amato

STATE UNIVERSITY OF NEW YORK PRESS

Published by
State University of New York Press, Albany

For information, address State University of New York Press
State University Plaza, Albany, NY 12246

Cover illustration by a slew of system mishaps.

Production by Cathleen Collins
Marketing by Fran Keneston

Library of Congress Cataloging-in-Publication Data

Amato, Joe, 1955–
    Bookend : anatomies of a virtual self / Joe Amato.
        p.   cm. — (SUNY series, postmodern culture)
    Includes bibliographical references.
    ISBN 0-7914-3401-X ISBN 0-7914-3402-8 (pbk.)
    1. American literature—20th century—History and criticism—
Theory, etc. 2. Postmodernism (Literature)—United States.
I. Title. II. Series: SUNY series in postmodern culture.
PS228.P68A43   1996
810.9′0054—dc21   96–47126
                                                        CIP

10 9 8 7 6 5 4 3 2 1

Technique is neither identical with form nor yet wholly independent of it. It is, properly, the skill with which the elements constituting form are managed. Otherwise it is show-off or a virtuosity separated from expression.

Significant advances in technique occur, therefore, in connection with efforts to solve problems that are not technical but that grow out of the need for new modes of experience. This statement is as true of esthetic arts as of the technological.

John Dewey, Art as Experience

CONTENTS

ACKNOWLEDGMENTS

The acknowledgments are scattered throughout, some by counterexample.

There are lots & lots of people out there without whose love & support I'd be lost. For them, then, & especially, for Kass Fleisher.

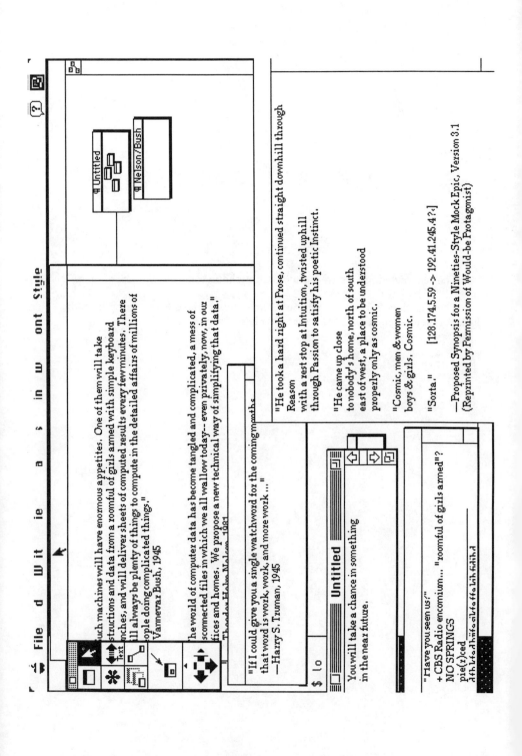

INTRODUCTION

The World's Body as Information Network

Without invention nothing is well spaced,
unless the mind change, unless
the stars are new measured, according
to their relative positions, the
line will not change, the necessity
will not matriculate: unless there is
a new mind there cannot be a new
line, the old will go on
repeating itself with recurring
deadliness: without invention
nothing lies under the witch-hazel
bush, the alder does not grow from among
the hummocks margining the all
but spent channel of the old swale,
the small foot-prints
of the mice under the overhanging
tufts of the bunch-grass will not
appear: without invention the line
will never again take on its ancient
divisions when the word, a supple word,
lived in it, crumbled now to chalk.[1]

---

1. William Carlos Williams, *Paterson* (New York: New Directions, 1963) 50. This excerpt from Book 2, first published 1948. For QuickStart, please proceed directly to first (or second, or . . .) anatomy.

William Carlos Williams's project in *Paterson* turned on the image of a figural human body pried open to reveal both a new urban discourse and a "new mind," a mind reflexively discovered in and through its attempt to reinvent and re-embody the poetic line. For Williams, there could be "no poetry of distinction without formal invention" (139).[2] In the above excerpt from *Paterson*, Williams's formulation of "invention" invokes disclosure—"the witch-hazel/bush"—as well as discovery, that which might be found to lie "under" it, an imaginative effort potentially buttressed by fact. That this excerpt, written in lines, consists of a series of four paratactic units (bound by colons), together comprising what reads, in effect (and largely owing to Williams's use of anaphora), as a long, hypotactic sentence, further suggests that Williams's "invention" is properly construed neither as a paean to the lyric nor as testament to the prevalence of prosody, but as encompassing a creative affirmation: that language provides the hybrid site upon and within which the "necessity" of contemporary experience may offset the "recurring deadliness" of "the old."

For Williams, both "the old" and new forms were to be regarded as technologically informed. "[I]t is in the intimate form," Williams had written in 1944, "that works of art achieve their exact meaning, in which they most resemble the machine" (139). Despite what we may now view as the particularly postmodern excesses of *Paterson*, Williams's poetic machine, as he conceived it, functioned as "any other machine," with "no part" that could be construed "redundant" (138). His poetics, however concretely bound up with *things*, was conditioned by a strong sense of elegance; hence "beauty" for him became that which "in a single object resolves our complex feelings of propriety" (138). Williams regarded poetry as the "machine which drives" prose, "pruned to a perfect economy," having "a physical more than a literary character." Poetry, as one of the arts, was hardly to be understood as a metaphysical matter: "Let the metaphysical take care of itself," Williams urged, "the arts have nothing to do with it" (138).

But this is, after all, Williams at his most ardently technological. As Lisa M. Steinman has argued, Williams indeed shared with Marianne Moore the belief that "poets might use technology both literally and to define an aesthetic that would be more relevant to their age than the aesthetic of nineteenth-century poetry" (47).[3] And yet these modernists likewise "deplored" the wholesale advocacy of "technological modernity" and its commodities "as the cure for all America's ills" (48). For

---

2. See Williams's introduction to *The Wedge*, *The Poetics of The New American Poetry*, ed. Donald Allen and Warren Tallman, (New York: Grove, 1973). Page numbers from this edition.

3. Lisa M. Steinman, *Made in America: Science, Technology, and American Modernist Poets* (New Haven: Yale UP, 1987). Cecelia Tichi discusses the social, cultural, and biographical underpinnings of Williams's "kinetic poetics" in *Shifting Gears: Technology, Literature, Culture in Modernist America* (Chapel Hill: U of North Carolina P, 1987); see "Machines Made of Words," 230–88. Tichi's account throws a somewhat more optimistic light over Williams's technological enthusiasm.

Williams, this led ultimately to an ambivalent view of the relationship between the machine and art. One could, as Steinman indicates, "force Williams' poetic to one possible conclusion," that "knowledge, language, poems, plants, and men are structurally similar, and their structural essence is best described by analogy to machines and technological products" (96). However, despite his frequent assertions, as above, in favor of a machine-poem analogy, Williams was never "fully comfortable with this view to which his acceptance of a certain style seemed to commit him" (96). As Steinman argues, his "struggle itself provides the mirror to modernity in search of which his career began," a struggle whose associated problems "are still with us" (112).

Times have changed, machines have changed. In the intervening half-century or so, many have modified, built upon, responded to, resisted, or simply tried to ignore the agenda Williams and other modernists set for themselves. Perhaps the most elaborate extension and reworking of Williams's poetics is to be found in Charles Olson's critical-poetic project.[4] Self-avowedly building on the work of Williams and Ezra Pound, Olson constructed his theory of "projective verse" by attending to the relationship among the various "objects" of the poem—"all the syllables and all the lines . . . managed in their relations to each other," what Olson termed the "field" (55).[5] Not unlike many of the modernists, Olson viewed the introduction of that more traditionally conceived print(ing) machine—the typewriter—as crucial to the enactment of this new verse form. "It is the advantage of the typewriter," Olson explained, "that, due to its rigidity and its space precisions, it can, for a poet, indicate exactly the breath, the pauses, the suspensions even of syllables, the juxtapositions even of parts of phrases, which he intends" (57). For Olson, the more structured typewritten space pushed compositional entropy uphill, in effect, permitting the creative process to begin at a potentially more productive and speech-centered datum. "It is time we picked the fruits of the experiments of Cummings, Pound, Williams," Olson asserted, "each of whom has, after his way, already used the machine as a scoring to his composing, as a script to its vocalization" (58). For Olson, this more formal "open verse" would enable a more profound poetic experience, one predicated on the notion that "speech is the

---

4. Space forbids (!) that I attempt an overview of the complex modulations of poetic practice that have characterized the intervening decades. Readers would do well to measure whatever historical assertions I offer here against Jed Rasula's erudite, stunningly comprehensive treatment of American poetry and its institutions, *The American Poetry Wax Museum: Reality Effects, 1940–1990* (Urbana: NCTE, 1996); and Alan Golding's careful, cogent study, *From Outlaw to Classic: Canons in American Poetry* (Madison: U of Wisconsin P, 1995).

5. Charles Olson, *Human Universe and Other Essays*, ed. Donald Allen, (New York: Grove, 1967), esp. "Human Universe," 3–15, "The Resistance," 48–49, and "Projective Verse," 51–61. For an excellent, detailed discussion of Olson's reformulation of modernist impulses, see Don Byrd, *Charles Olson's* Maximus (Urbana: U of Illinois P, 1980) 3–26.

'solid' of verse, is the secret of the poem's energy" (56). This "secret" is realized, empowered within the field. As Don Byrd observes, "it is space as a source of energy that replaces for Olson the tradition of Pound and Eliot" (15; see note 5).

Secrets, energies, and the like generally suggest a ghost in the machine, and indeed Olson, unlike Williams, was clearly not averse to metaphysical speculation, as regards either the poetic or the biolinguistic. Writing in 1951, Olson articulated his vision—his "guess at a way to restore to man some of his lost relevance" (9)—in what many may find even in these times utterly breathtaking, and breathtakingly ingenuous, terms:

> What happens at the skin is more like than different from what happens within. . . . Here again, as throughout experience, the law remains, form is not isolated from content. . . . Which is why the man said, he who possesses rhythm, possesses the universe. And why art is the only twin life has—its only valid metaphysic. Art does not seek to describe but to enact. And if man is once more to possess intent in his life, and to take up the responsibility implicit in his life, he has to comprehend his own process as intact, from outside, by way of his skin, in, and by his own powers of conversion, out again. (10)

As Olson puts it in an extraordinary couple of pages entitled "The Resistance," human kind "came here by an intolerable way" and must accept the challenge of mortality as the "root act" of this arrival and subsequent (individual) departure (*Human Universe* 48). "It is his [man's] body that is his answer," he writes, "his body intact and fought for, the absolute of his organism in its simplest terms, this structure evolved by nature, repeated in each act of birth, the animal man . . . " (48). Olson is a primitivist precisely to the extent of his desire to recuperate and revitalize the human organism's response to such an "absolute"—"its fragile mortal force its old eternity, resistance" (49)—through the experience of a vitally present and process-based language. "This is eternity. This now. This foreshortened span," he writes (48), and the present finitude becomes for Olson the vital measure against which we are to seek out our requisite words.[6]

This is a tall order, especially in the wake of poststructuralism. The spatial rigidities of the typewriter have given way to ostensibly more fluid, but equally regulated, electronic spaces, spaces which themselves reflect and participate in a less stable, more fragmented, more multivariate conception of public and private consciousness. And this, in turn, requires a more pluralistic response to poetic matters than Olson, writing during the cold war era, could muster.

---

6. For insight into the relationship between Olson's and Robert Creeley's poetics as these relate to the body (with useful digressions on the poetry of Edward Dorn and Robert Duncan, and the philosophy of Maurice Merleau-Ponty), see Stephen Fredman's important study, *Poet's Prose: The Crisis in American Verse*, 2nd ed. (Cambridge: Cambridge UP, 1990) 89–100.

My project in the pages that follow is an attempt to renegotiate the creative legacy of Williams and Olson in fin de siècle America, to re-member our bodies as we encounter the ubiquitous and potentially dismembering electronic interface, that passage into what Michael Joyce has contextualized in contemporary terms as a "city of text."[7] Williams and Olson: For my purposes, I might just as soon have chosen Stein, Pound, Zukofsky, Riding—any number of innovators within the spectrum of twentieth-century American poetry. My choice reflects a provisional beginning, a place to begin again. Like Williams's, my project will invoke a renewed attention to the line—but to the *virtual* line, the line that augurs a digital world—as a means through which to establish a renewed appreciation of the relationship between the conventions of old and new discursive form. Like Olson's, my project will map the human body as a construction upon the field—but upon the *virtual* field, the field that augurs a digital world—in order to bring modulations of spatiality to bear on human aspiration. If such a project is not entirely without poetic precedent, neither is it isolated from the history of dominant critical apparatus operating under the aegis of modernism.

• • • •

Published in 1938, John Crowe Ransom's foundational New Critical articulation of "the world's body" may today be understood as an attempt to resolve Depression-era anxieties over Baudelaire's perennial humbug of modernity. By situating what he regarded as the sensuous and concrete affectivities of poetry at the crossroads of an individualized human experience and a progressively alienating social enterprise, Ransom hoped to offset the encroachment of modern times. As Terry Eagleton has observed, Ransom believed that "scientific rationalism was ravaging the 'aesthetic life' of the old South," hence that the way out of such rationalism was to advocate the presumably more "contemplative" and "disinterested" mode of poetic discourse in an effort to restore to lived experience a measure of near-religious "humility."[8] Ransom's advocacy of a "physical poetry," one attentive to "physical things," however "impure," gives the lie to a purely theological *critical* motive, of course, and his distinction between things and ideas situates him, ironically, on the verge of a particularly positivistic ontology.[9] Whether contemplative or meditative in character, finally, Ransom's "physical poetry" calls for a phenomenological shift on the part both of poet and reader and a subsequent view toward

7. Michael Joyce , "New Teaching: Toward a Pedagogy for a New Cosmology," *Computers and Composition* 9.2 (April 1992): 7–16.

8. Terry Eagleton, *Literary Theory: An Introduction* (Minneapolis: U of Minnesota P, 1983) 46–47.

9. John Crowe Ransom, *The World's Body* (New York: Scribner's, 1938) 111–42.

what is objectified either as external or internal, in order to produce or behold "images so whole and clean that they resist the catalysis of thought."

Ontologies notwithstanding, if we recognize today the peculiarly agrarian, nostalgic, and reactionary elements both of Ransom's "world" and "body"—and can therefore actively address, in our texts and in our classrooms, such a parochial and ultimately reductive worldview by attending to the ideological machinery evident in such work—it is perhaps yet the case that most of us remain ill equipped to interrogate Ransom's distinction between the poetic and the scientific. This aspect of "the world's body," despite a half-century interim of sustained critical activity, has in fact been inverted by the incursion and proliferation of those systems collectively described in commonplace terms as "information technologies." Thanks to the politics and innovations of scientific and technological practices, it would seem that global networks have managed to displace more poetic imperatives, and this is to be regretted, not because Ransom was correct in his evaluation of poetic discourse, but because poetic practice may in fact represent a way to rethink the scientific and technological to yield more responsive and responsible social practices. When measured against human technological practices, practices that remain at once manifestly material and political even as they engage the symbolic, the various living bodies of the world have, in effect, suffered dis-member-ment to varying degrees, a literal and metaphorical disembodiment perhaps best understood in social terms as the reflex action of local inhabitants thrust into, or excluded from, the global alliances and neighborhoods that have materialized since the Second World War. Proximity, finally, provokes territorial valuations, xenophobic anxieties. And, like any city, a city of text must unavoidably nurture a criminal element.

This suggests a rather extensive critical agenda, and one fully resonant with the development of the very technologies at issue, for to proceed *without* due regard for the advent of new technologies of articulation—hypermedia, for instance—would be to attempt to situate my feelings, and my body, somehow outside of what I perceive to be those cultural ebbs and flows that characterize contemporary social experience. The development of electronic media, as I see and feel it, prompts me to conclude that it will simply no longer do to consider the articulation of such feelings as disconnected either from the contents or the forms of technology. If our engagement with the technologies of our times effects a corresponding alteration in our sense of self, individual and collective, it is likewise the case that it is only through our presumed understanding of the networks involved in our self-shaping—networks of constraint, desire, and commitment—that we pursue our livelihoods, and our dreams.

It is time to call the various bluffs of what Jay David Bolter has so aptly referred to as this "late age of print," and my work will, I hope, contribute to the sustained articulation of remembered and embodied worlds—worlds congenial to the development and sustenance of various and emerging forms of life on this durable, yet paradoxically delicate, planet.[10] Negotiating such a wager will resituate in lasting ways the tacit technologies of the book, bringing them to a provisional end and ushering in a new beginning: henceforth, linearly coherent, cover-to-cover, quasi-hermetic text will continue to metamorphose as electronic media gain momentum, and these changes will change the shape of all text.[11] If we understand such changes in terms of their effect upon the composition process itself, it becomes clear that poetic license—license to explore and interrogate new forms—provides the lasting imprimatur for pursuing a rearticulation of written spatiality. Further, because the anatomies of a virtual subject documented herein reflect in large part my experience *as a writer* during this transitional period—and are in this sense autographical—I feel somewhat justified, albeit decidedly optimistic, in believing that this my bookend may support a more open and creatively critical scholastic forum, and perhaps a more humane technology.[12]

• • • •

Those who seek herein for a programmatic solution to current turmoils are bound to be a bit disappointed, for these harbingers of the book's end have emerged from

---

10. Jay David Bolter, *Writing Space: The Computer, Hypertext, and the History of Writing* (Hillsdale: Erlbaum, 1991). This book (and corresponding hypertext floppy) became in effect *the* rallying cry for many academics (like myself) who felt that electronic media augured something new under the sun. Though now somewhat dated in outlook (owing to the enormous amount of commentary published since) it nonetheless provides solid historical perspective for a discussion of electronic form and forum.

11. George P. Landow's *Hypertext: The Convergence of Contemporary Critical Theory and Technology* (Johns Hopkins UP, 1992) is still perhaps the best single overview to date of the more theoretical implications of hypermedia technologies, despite its relative neglect of poetic practice. See also the essays in George P. Landow, ed., *Hyper/Text/Theory* (Johns Hopkins UP, 1994); and Marjorie Perloff's ruminations regarding the various formal tensions that have emerged as information age poets come ftf with electronic text, in *Radical Artifice: Writing Poetry in the Age of Media* (U of Chicago P, 1991). And for a thorough (reception-theory-based, feminist) critique of the more liberatory claims associated with hypertext per se, see Mary Elizabeth Hocks, "Technotropes of Liberation: Reading Hypertext in the Age of Theory," diss., U of Illinois at Urbana-Champaign, 1994.

12. I cannot emphasize enough the extent to which feminist discourse—particularly the work of Donna Haraway—has influenced my orientation toward the body/machine interface. In critical terms, I regard my project as an allied, albeit tangential, endeavor. See, for example, Haraway's oft-cited essay, "A Manifesto for Cyborgs: Science, Technology, and Socialist Feminism in the 1980s," *Socialist Review* 80 (Mar.–Apr. 1985): 65–107. I have found the work of Michel de Certeau most helpful in teasing out (though not reconciling) the con- and crosscurrent logics of disparate discourses; see *Heterologies: Discourse on the Other*, trans. Brian Massumi, Theory and History of Lit., 17 (Minneapolis: U of Minnesota P, 1986). And the promise of revitalized language practices as these may correspond to a re-visionary poetics is perhaps nowhere better imagined than in Don Byrd's sweeping *The Poetics of the Common Knowledge* (New York: State U of New York P, 1993).

8

my own very intimate encounters with technology. They have primarily to do with the political, ontological, and narratological grounding of positivistic, epistemological, and empirical modes of inquiry that, in retrospect, constituted a network of beliefs, values, and practices—a pretext, in short—for the institutional constraints under which I once worked, conditioning in countless ways my day-to-day experiences and aspirations. Whatever one chooses to make of "reality," it is indeed an intricate affair, and I lay no claim to having rendered things, or words, more discrete as a result of my anatomies. By embracing a world of information through a meaningfully disjoint body of text—print or electronic, electronic to print—the paradox of authorship and identity is amplified, the subroutine becomes a routine: one writes oneself only to discover the degree to which one has already been written. And therein lie our choices. This represents a peculiar sort of literacy, finally, for an understanding of the ways in which writing technologies create the possibilities for a variety of subjects and objects is a measure of one's ability to rearticulate the formal conventions of writing, to reread and rewrite, recenter or decenter, reenergize oneself with an understanding of the liabilities and perturbations inherent to such active, environmentally contingent, regenerative processing.

And a thing more: in composing these anatomies, these cutups, these disquisitions on mind and heart, body and soul—which open to an inkling of insight into a cosmic (and comic) consciousness born of social experience—I have come to a renewed appreciation of how style may, under the right conditions, reveal substance. Anatomies of the self as a virtual subject are congenial to the demands of this space in time in which we find ourselves writing, this early age of *molecular* reproduction and replication, an age of fully digitalized stylistic appropriation. By hyperactively de-optimizing discourse through the use of dissonant and reflexive strategies present in our current print | electronic culture, I expect to push functionalist and reductivist views of language to the limits of their descriptive and prescriptive powers.[13] And my expectation here should be taken less as methodological pre-text than as an ex post facto presumption as to reception.

•　　•　　•　　•

---

13. Why do I feel compelled here to insert a citation? What is it makes me want to resist? Have I invoked a masculinist, evangelical, positivistic oligarchy? Were I to acknowledge my complicity in the very activities I find suspect—particularly the (post)modernist critical edifice—it might be that much more evident that I surely have no intention of bullshitting either my readers or myself as to my ability to legislate categories such as electronic and—by counterexample?—print discourse. And yet it seems to me apropos of these postmodern times to attempt to account for one's reading and writing convictions. That I regard my work as counter-academic on at least several fronts owes something to the sorts of creative transgressions one finds in the work of, say, Robert Burton, Jack Spicer, Roland Barthes, Raymond Federman, Mary Daly, Paul Feyerabend, Ihab Hassan,

An updated version of what some might regard as primitivist aesthetics (after Olson) or formalist media cant (after McLuhan) is likely to be met with much (micro?)resistance by today's hipper and hippest scholars without at least a provisional qualification in light of that incipient elitism which characterizes all modernist, or crypto-modernist, agenda.

Much to my chagrin, it is unlikely that common folk, however one construes such a tag, will in fact be afforded the opportunity of reading this text. When I think of "common folk," I invariably have in mind my father, a man who worked for hourly (union and nonunion) wages his entire life as a furniture finisher. No college, a veteran, first-generation American, a craftsman by this country's standards: he would indeed have had, as he might have put it, a *helluva* time with my book. That he would have worked his way through parts of it, though, belies the fact that access to such texts is in large part a matter of preexisting social strata.

Moreover, it is evident that the sort of thing I am after in these pages has much to do with a presumed response, not to the formal per se, but to those convolutions of formal expectation and formal invention that serve to highlight the rhetorical inadequacy and technological blindness of all form-content dualisms.[14] Formally speaking, I would venture that there is much in this text that is likely to strike readers as at once traditional and "new," whether or not I have made it that way. "Newness" is, finally, itself a function of the ways through which social technologies such as print and TV conventionalize expectations; this is hardly a one-way, cause-effect matter, for people of whatever cultural or social status are subject(ed) to experiences that are only partially inflected by the workings of media. Yet the latent emancipatory and participatory promises inherent in my project *do* bring with them a McLuhanistic reliance on the efficacy of technological means to (oftentimes) nontechnological ends.

Gregory Ulmer, Gloria Anzaldúa, Scott McCloud, Rachel Blau DuPlessis, Johanna Drucker, and the TINAC electronic arts collective (a disparate grouping, to be sure), suggesting that current critical exigencies, regarding which I am by historical fiat an unwitting co-conspirator, will make of any such creative categorization an exercise in re-creation, extra-vagance; as the latter's etymology would imply, a "wandering beyond," even to the point of self-indulgence. My project may thus be justifiably viewed as extravagant (if non-Frostian), oversaturated with the generic, incorporating what it will of the consumer-oriented, pseudo-libertarian, body-wrap agenda underwriting so much of our suburban, preprocessed, noisily aerobic, commercial-fetishistic media environment (the distinction between mass and popular culture is not lost on me). I would not find it odd were such work to be critiqued as *tentative, uneven*—a partial disclosure. But there is no getting around, finally, getting around. . . . The real issue(s) here may in fact have primarily to do with publishing (un)realities—the appearance of this text on an academic press series instead of the customary small-press publication and distribution of such formal maneuvers (this introduction excepted).

14. I owe most of this paragraph to Andrew Ross's superbly balanced critique of McLuhan's formalist (modernist) underpinning in *No Respect: Intellectuals and Popular Culture* (New York: Routledge, 1989) 114–34.

I might simply observe that "technology" and "media" may serve as umbrella terms for one another (as they, in fact, often do in this text) only at the expense of reducing compulsory and discriminating social practices to a *form* of passive or active, social or individual, hot or cold, oppositional or conciliatory, intellectual or anti-intellectual, educational or entertaining *interaction*. However, given the sort of social ferment I take to be indicative of the times, this is a liability with which any writer working today must contend. That one might occasionally wax populist, for instance, is a litmus both of streetwise conformism *and* georgic empiricism.

•   •   •   •

The critical forum has itself in recent years begun to sing the praises of its own reform. Though this forum has never been a monolithic entity, it nonetheless operates within a preset professional context, hence one might expect a method-ological commonality to inhere even across ostensibly disparate agenda, largely owing to the highly regulated circulation of negotiable intellectual currency. As an example, and one particularly pertinent to my project, the collection of essays edited by H. Aram Veeser entitled *The New Historicism* illustrates the degree to which the poetic has become a readily appropriable and powerfully convenient category through which to promulgate a (presumably) more openly creative, con-jectural historiography.[15]

The opening essays, in fact, by Stephan Greenblatt and Louis A. Montrose, though somewhat opposed to each other in conceptual outlook, nonetheless bear homage to poetry in explicitly titular terms: the title of Greenblatt's piece, "Towards a Poetics of Culture"; of Montrose's, "Professing the Renaissance: The Poetics and Politics of Culture." Simply on the basis of these titles, one might con-clude that a poetics—as distinguished from a poetry—of culture is somehow desirable and that it would seem to be a difficult but necessary objective to work "toward." However, rather than detail my reservations regarding the use of *poetic* in either of these two essays—both of which make valid and valuable contribu-tions to their field—I would like instead to focus on Hayden White's more pithy concluding piece, "New Historicism: A Comment." White elucidates the reasons why the New Historicists give offense to the prevailing critical orthodoxies. They would appear to be quite a marginalized group: "the New Historicists offend against the formal tenets of an older but still powerful New Criticism"; "against the newer, Post-structuralist versions of formalism"; against "historians in gen-eral"; and against "historians and traditional literary scholars alike" (294).

But for White, what finally presents the "possibility of genuinely principled disagreement" between the New Historicists and "both traditional 'bourgeois' historians and their Marxist counterparts"—what gives real offense, in other

---

15. H. Aram Veeser, ed., *The New Historicism* (New York: Routledge, 1989).

11

words—results from a shared program to "conceptualize the *syntagmatic* dimension of the history of literature and by extension the history of both culture and society as well" (299). Utilizing Roman Jakobson's linguistic model, and elaborating on Montrose's earlier essay, White argues that New Historicists have foregrounded the " 'poetic' and the 'metalinguistic' functions of language" (300). And because, for Jakobson, the poetic and the metalinguistic, as alternate syntagmatic processes, "are in diametrical opposition to each other" (qtd. in White 300), this leads to a rather chaotic notion of "*historical sequentiality*" (300; White's italics). Formalist historians evidently prefer a more " 'code-like,' less 'poetic' " model of historical change (301).[16] "[O]n my understanding of the matter at least," White writes,

> the New Historicists have advanced the notion of a "cultural poetics" and by extension a "historical poetics" as a means of identifying those aspects of historical sequences that conduce to the breaking, revision, or weakening of the dominant codes . . . prevailing at specific times and places in history. Whence their interest in what appears to be the episodic, anecdotal, contingent, exotic, abjected, or simply uncanny aspects of the historical record. These aspects of history can be deemed "poetic"—in the sense of "creative" (rather than that of "fanciful" or "imaginary")—in that they appear to escape, transcend, contravene, undermine, or contest the rules, laws, and principles of the modes of social organization . . . predominating at the time of their appearance. In this respect, they can be said to resemble poetic speech which, even though it may contravene the rules of both grammar and logic, not only *has* meaning, but also always implicitly challenges the canonical rules of linguistic expression prevailing at the time of its utterance. (301)

It would seem, then, that what we are dealing with here is either (1) an incredibly impoverished notion of poetics—for how, precisely, might New Historicism *itself* "escape" or "transcend"—or "appear to"—those poetic conventions which have been "deemed 'poetic'" by the community of poets, a discourse community that has long since responded to the Jakobsonian model, and without whose artifacts and practices all of this talk of "offense" is merely a matter of objectionable content purged of any formal, stylistically substantive *poetic* controversy save for the fact that—is it hundreds?—of New Historicists have decided to violate past historiographic practice by adopting a more literary perspective? (and I simply cannot refrain from noting the persistent quotes with which White chooses to demarcate

---

16. White's analysis is actually more complex than I have indicated, entailing a rather intriguing subsumption of the diachronic by the synchronic. Cartesian dichotomies, in any case, provide no way out.

both *poetic* and *creative*);[17] or (2) a collapse of the distinctions between the poetic-creative and the historiographical, in which event all poets would be well advised to rethink their (fictive) audiences accordingly.

In short, and despite White's perceptive and well-intentioned analysis of one aspect of contemporary historical inquiry, there is no attempt made to reference those practices or texts endemic to the discourse community represented by the community of poets—itself a highly variegated institution. If item (2) indeed represents current trends, it is likewise evident that a discussion of poetics, at least as practiced by New Historians who concur with Montrose à la White, has somehow managed to sidestep the complex matter of aesthetic innovation as this relates both to critical poiesis and critical evaluation.[18] Use of the standard genres of literary criticism—novel, anecdote, and so forth—whether historically discrete or contextually resonant, has in general been allowed to serve as a surrogate for sustained analysis of the contemporary adoption and enactment of such forms, a particularly modernist (critical) strategy to the extent that rhetorical aplomb masks a politics of stylistic appropriation.[19] But this is a modernism purged of Olson's ensuing problematic; a modernism that, as recently as the early seventies, could dispense with as central a figure as Gertrude Stein; a modernism devoid of

---

17. A fuller account would elaborate on Jakobson's efforts as founder of the Prague school of (structural) linguistics (with due regard for the influence of Saussure's work), his critical contribution to the Russian formalist movement, and this movement's affinities to modernist poetics, especially as articulated by Eliot. Helpful historical perspective on formalist literary theory and practice is provided in Frank Lentricchia's *After the New Criticism* (Chicago: U of Chicago P, 1980).

18. To be fair, Montrose, for his part, seems to intuit the complexities associated with his assertion that "not only the poet but also the critic exists in history" ("Professing the Renaissance," Veeser 24). As he observes, the "conviction that formal and historical concerns are not opposed but rather are inseparable," one "implicit in" a "'Cultural Poetics'" project, is "perhaps not yet adequately articulated or theorized"(17).

19. In attempting to identify what he refers to as the "relays" operating between "market culture" and "machine culture"—those social and institutional practices and discourses that work to coordinate bodies and machines—Mark Seltzer reaches a similar conclusion regarding the "logic of equivalence" that underwrites so much (though of course not all) cultural criticism. "By this logic," he writes, "the very notion of a 'cultural poetics' is already a tautological one" (84). See Mark Seltzer, *Bodies and Machines* (New York: Routledge, 1992), esp. 45–90. Seltzer's study of turn-of-the-century American literature and culture resonates nicely with current body-machine interface arguments, providing historical correspondence for my occasionally rather vigorous appeal to "new" materialisms owing to contemporary writing technologies. In his words, "such a becoming visible of the technology of writing in machine culture risks making visible the links between the materiality of writing and the making of persons, and thus the internal relations between persons and machines" (79).

much of the more liberal and liberatory discourse produced by so many of its vital, and now marginalized or forgotten, constituents.[20]

This is hardly surprising: White himself has forged his own, specifically tropological agenda with more than an eye toward "the principal modalities of figuration, identified in post-Renaissance rhetorical theory as the 'master tropes' (Kenneth Burke's phrase) of metaphor, metonymy, synecdoche, and irony."[21] But what were Burke's "master tropes" if not, in effect, a reaffirmation of those selfsame rhetorical practices and tropic exchanges with which so many modernist critics and poets of that era sought to distinguish between what Burke had in 1931 cautiously referred to as "'pure'" and "applied" (i.e., more intensively commodi-

---

20. Again, my remarks here are only cursory. For refreshing alternatives to the traditional modernist edifice, see Cary Nelson, *Repression and Recovery: Modern American Poetry and the Politics of Cultural Memory 1910–1945* (Madison: U of Wisconsin P, 1989); Jerome Rothenberg and Pierre Joris, Vol. 1 of *Poems for the Millennium, From Fin-de-Siècle to Negritude,* (Berkeley: U of California P, 1995); Maria Damon's thought-provoking reworking of the "marginal," *The Dark End of the Street: Margins in American Vanguard Poetry* (Minneapolis: U of Minnesota P, 1993); and Miriam Bratu Hansen's ongoing articulation of a "popular modernism," elaborated in "America, Paris, the Alps: Kracauer (and Benjamin) on Cinema and Modernity," *Cinema and the Invention of Modern Life,* ed. Leo Charney and Vanessa R. Schwartz (Berkeley: U of California P, 1995). Regarding those "Regional Differences" at work in shaping the poetic practices of contemporary American poets: readers might consult the eight interviews in *Ottotole* 3 (Spring 1989), which in addition afford some insight into how poets today may construe alternatives to a univocal poetics; also, the collection of language poetry-writing edited by Ron Silliman, *In the American Tree* (Orono, ME: National Poetry Foundation, 1986), anthologized along east-west coordinates (which at times reveals the *absence* of such differences!). I might add that the formal-institutional conventions against which poets define their work are often as restrictive and exclusionary as those of historians; my point is not to endorse one or another set of practices or communities (despite my occasional smartassedness), and I am well aware of the difficulties of addressing *any* such "group" in monolithic terms. Yet I feel it fair and necessary to observe that the critical establishment, so (and self-) defined, has by and large effected an ultimately fiberless appropriation of terms with little regard for poets and poetry (an ironic development, given current residual hegemonies, hegemonies initiated by the New Critical poet-critics; see Rasula and Golding, note 4 above). I would emphasize also that (white) North American poets throughout this century have in particular failed to confront their own appropriative stance vis-à-vis the stereotypes of racial discourse. A good place to begin an appraisal of American poetry's vexed relationship with race is Aldon Lynn Nielsen's incisive (and often damning) *Reading Race: White American Poets and the Racial Discourse in the Twentieth Century* (Athens, GA: U of Georgia P, 1988). For an excellent survey of the current shortcomings of cyberspace in racial/ethnic terms, see Joe Lockard, "Virtual Whiteness and Narrative Diversity," *Undercurrent* 4 (Spring 1996), online, World Wide Web, <http://darkwing.uoregon.edu/~heroux/uc4/4-lockard.html>; and for a cogent critique of the celebrated multiplicity of cyberspace identity formations, one that stresses the pertinence of African-American criticism and literature to cyberspace discourse, see Kali Tal, "Life Behind the Screen," *Wired* 4.10 (October 1996): 134, 136.

21. Hayden White, *Tropics of Discourse: Essays in Cultural Criticism* (Baltimore: Johns Hopkins UP, 1978) 5.

fied) literatures?[22] There is in fact nothing new about this redistribution of the poetic; literary critics of one stripe or another have been attentive to poetic practice since the ancients. Yet if the critical world has grown increasingly—perhaps debilitatingly—postmodern, it has done so, evidently, by dehistoricizing its modernist underpinning, thereby encouraging a tacit discrimination against all that is not properly modern.

• • • •

The written representation of technological objects, processes, systems, and practices often obscures the fact that writing is itself a technology, hence that the imperatives and constraints of such writing technologies have in fact preconditioned such writing practices. But written discourse may resist deterministic critical machinery through an engagement *with* such machinery, much as what David Porush has termed "cybernetic fictions" at first glance "appear to be machines but foil the simple production of sense, the blueprinting, that mechanism promises."[23] Throughout my musings, I accept as an operating premise the view that the writing process itself reflects an active and constitutive engagement with environment. "[S]ince we exist in language," write Humberto R. Maturana and Francisco J. Varela, "the domains of discourse that we generate become part of our domain of existence and constitute part of the environment in which we conserve identity and adaptation."[24] One such environment is that of *cyberspace*— the term currently in vogue to denote both a digitized environmental simulation created by computer-generated impulses and the metaphorical space of data processing. Equipped with a full array of computer hardware and software, then, and with the assumption of even a few "domains of discourse," we language-bound creatures may infer that "identity" and "adaptation" are hardly discrete

22. Cf. Kenneth Burke, *Counter-Statement* (1931; Berkeley: U of California P, 1968) 89–90. Burke here is characteristically judicious in his (literary) observations. "Our program," he writes, "is simply to point out that the criterion of 'usefulness' has enjoyed much more prestige than its underlying logic merited." His "Four Master Tropes" appears as an appendix in Kenneth Burke, *A Grammar of Motives* (Berkeley: U of California P, 1945) 503–17.

23. David Porush, *The Soft Machine: Cybernetic Fiction* (New York: Methuen, 1985) 70. Kenneth Burke's summary dismissal of Gertrude Stein's *Geography and Plays* as "Engineering with Words" (the title of his review) reveals the degree to which even a perceptive critical intellect might fail to grasp the value of such "mechanical" (literary) experimentation. See Kenneth Burke, "Engineering with Words" (the title of his 1923 review), *Critical Essays on Gertrude Stein*, ed. Michael J. Hoffman (Boston: Hall, 1986) 42–45; originally published 1923.

24. Humberto R. Maturana and Francisco J. Varela, *The Tree of Knowledge: The Biological Roots of Human Understanding* (Boston: New Science Library/Shambhala, 1988) 234.

entities and are subject to regulation only as a function of our interaction with environmental constraints.

Karen Burke LeFevre has demonstrated persuasively how invention becomes a collaboratively (and collectively) social act. Moreover, its shared material basis marks it as an activity implicating the individual in an institutionally codified biological-machine matrix. If we further assume, with Eric Havelock, that the transition from oral to print culture in fact separated the "knower from the known," the transition from print to cyberculture may be seen as potentially both a rending and a mending: while obscuring distinctions among knowledge, information, and lived experience, these technologies nonetheless provide geographically remote communities of knowers/users with (near) synchronous venues through which to reinvent, reenact, and disperse such distinctions.[25] Such reenactments must make the matter of bodily bodies both source and site of contention, primarily because, as Allucquere Rosanne Stone has it,

> Cyberspace developers foresee a time when they will be able to forget about the body. But it is important to remember that virtual community originates in, and must return to, the physical. No refigured virtual body, no matter how beautiful, will slow the death of a cyberpunk with AIDS. Even in the age of the technosocial subject, life is lived through bodies.[26]

A lived and living body correlative to a field poetics signifies not simply language as a medium, but language as a commentary on linguistic processing. Field theory in twentieth-century *science* impacted upon theories of language to the extent that

---

25. See Karen Burke LeFevre, *Invention as a Social Act* (Carbondale: Southern Illinois UP, 1987); and Eric Havelock, *Origins of Western Literacy* (Toronto: Ontario Inst. for Studies in Educ., 1976). For an excellent discussion of the relationship among orality, performance, and (print-induced) private ownership of knowledge, one that places the emergence of cyberculture within the context of socially transformative language technologies, see Doug Brent, "Oral Knowledge, Typographic Knowledge, Electronic Knowledge: Speculations on the History of Ownership," *EJOURNAL* 1.3 (1991): n. pag., online, World Wide Web, 30 July 1992. <http://www.hanover.edu/philos/ejournal/archive/ej-1-3.txt>.

26. Allucquere Rosanne Stone, "Will the Real Body Please Stand Up? Boundary Stories about Virtual Cultures," *Cyberspace: First Steps*, Michael Benedikt, ed., (Cambridge: MIT P, 1991) 113. The essays in this volume provide a stimulating starting point for discussion of cyberspace technologies. With regard to the relationship between poetry and cyberspace in particular, Marcos Novak waxes most poetic: "Cyberspace is poetry inhabited, and to navigate through it is to become a leaf on the wind of a dream." See Marcos Novak, "Liquid Architectures in *Cyberspace*," *Cyberspace*, esp. 227–29.

language had henceforth to be viewed, in the words of N. Katherine Hayles, as "part of the mediating field":

> To admit the field concept thus entails admitting that the self-referentiality of language is not accidental, but an essential consequence of speaking from within the field.[27]

A language that is self-referential inherently admits of multiple linguistic selves even as it challenges (referential) distinctions among language-users. Yet, deep structure or no, the mutability of feelings, emotions, tastes, intuitions and the like, wrought and circulated through culturally and socially specific symbolic practices, may well suggest a development within the corresponding linguistic field of a sufficient degree of morphological (pragmatic, semantic, phonetic, phonemic, semiotic) complexity to induce the emergence of new patterns of articulation. Whether "chaos" as an operational paradigm displaces or simply enhances the field concept is perhaps of less importance here than the underlying premise: only a sufficiently rich metaphorical pool permits such reflexive scrutiny, and only linguistic mechanisms varying with the evolving species can embrace all consequent bodily manifestations. In short: if virtual communities provide us with new ways of thinking about the sorts of creatures we are, and could become, language may accordingly be regarded in more modest, less restrictive terms. Neither Logos nor medium, the word, written and spoken, may play a more active role in helping to chart the path toward those discoveries and disclosures requisite to the development of healthy environments.[28]

•　　•　　•　　•

---

27. N. Katherine Hayles, *The Cosmic Web: Scientific Field Models and Literary Strategies in the Twentieth Century* (Ithaca: Cornell UP, 1984) 41; and see her more recent study of the "isomorphic" interrelations of newer chaos-based sciences, poststructural theory, and literature, *Chaos Bound: Orderly Disorder in Contemporary Literature and Science* (Ithaca: Cornell UP, 1990). The most ambitious attempt to date at bringing theories of complexity and self-organization to bear on various "ecologies of composition" (including electronic mail) is Margaret A. Syverson's "The Wealth of Reality: An Ecology of Composition," diss., U California at San Diego, 1994.

28. David Sewell's provocative examination of the Usenet Oracle phenomenon reconsiders the role of authorship in the construction of virtual worlds. For Sewell, these language games born of a hacker subculture provide evidence that "the computer's ability to create self-contained virtual worlds is beginning to affect what we traditionally call 'writing' or 'literature' as distinct from 'mere' game." See David Sewell, "The Usenet Oracle: Virtual Authors and Network Community," *EJOURNAL* 2.5 (1992): n. pag., online, World Wide Web, 19 Jan. 1993 <http:// www.hanover. edu/philos/ejournal/archive/cj-2-5.txt>. And for one of the earliest studies of what she calls (after Foucault) the "information panopticon" and its effect on online community, see Shoshana Zuboff, *In the Age of the Smart Machine* (New York: Basic Books, 1988), Chapter Ten.

My merging of a multitude of subjective categories—itself a consequence of the manipulation of (age-old) formal and technical conventions—has the effect of emphasizing the energetic and tactile qualities of media, the degree to which a hybrid compositional process (i.e., pixel to print) is just that—a material interplay of living and nonliving bodies, some perhaps more palpable than others.

This affords some insight into the ways in which more representational, less disjunctive, more seamless performances, however familiar or traditional, simulate an energyless information matrix. Much has been made of that corporate/government-sponsored recodifying of energy and its associated schemata that began shortly after the Second World War. The terms of nineteenth-century thermodynamics—entropy and the like—were found amenable to the formulations of this new science, and the technologies of information storage and retrieval were likewise afforded a valuable new paradigm against which experts and converts could presumably measure the rigor of their designs.[29] But what seems to me to have been given relatively short shrift in all of this has been the degree to which our society, a society ever more dependent upon (possibly nonrenewable) energy resources, has predicated its cultural, economic, and political status, not upon an understanding of information as a form of energy, but upon the premise, metaphorically and literally entertaining, that energy is merely one of a number of manifestations of information.

The recognition that information processing is enabled only as a consequence of energy expenditure—however efficient the microchip—has at least the advantage of calling one's attention to its necessarily depletable status in local, hence human, terms; such are the mandates of the first and second laws of thermodynamics and their corollaries. Conversely, to regard energy merely as a form of information invokes a popular mantra: information—like energy, neither created nor destroyed—emerges from a cosmological black hole in which we invest neither limbic energies nor financial dividends. This dream of a limitless, price-less spatial plenitude, the simulation of a multinational (and territorializing) omniscience that underwrites so many literary narratives, constitutes the teleological black box facilitating the design of cyberspace technologies and beckons perhaps to a dystopic destiny manifestly latent in our new age: one is empowered, or energized, precisely to the extent of one's access to an ice-cold, de-energized and manipulable cyberenvironment, a seamlessly perpetual and dynamically revers-

29. Jeremy Campbell's *Grammatical Man: Information, Entropy, Language, and Life* (New York: Simon, 1982) remains one of the best overviews of this conceptual alignment. A fascinating mélange of these matters may be found in Michel Serres's brief essay "The Origin of Language: Biology, Information Theory, and Thermodynamics," *Hermes: Literature, Science, Philosophy*, eds. J. V. Harari and D. F. Bell, (Baltimore: Johns Hopkins UP, 1982) 71–83. The emerging fields of cybernetics and information theory exerted a profound influence on research in the human sciences. For an account focusing on the period immediately following the Second World War (specifically, the Macy Conferences), see Steve J. Heims, *The Cybernetics Group* (Cambridge: MIT P, 1991).

ible stasis in which the distinctions between artificial and natural, living and non-living, real and unreal, literal and metaphorical, seem either no longer pertinent, or immanently recombinant. One might argue that, circumstances permitting, the circuit politic's postmortem would reveal a society rich in information, replete with divestiture, and—as a consequence of such sensory indulgence—utterly lacking in egalitarian initiative. Viewed in a somewhat more dramatic light, this zero energy datum brings us to the tether of pessimistic speculation: a worldwide biological, ecological, or economic collapse whose alleged victims' collective plight is less the result of social construction than of ideological, quasi-conspiratorial fabrication, a fabrication air-conditioning its financially privileged citizens into political stupor and leaving its underprivileged to their own survival devices.

Enter the cyborg: it would seem that we are all cybernetic organisms simply as a consequence of having been projected into an extensive world. All technologies, including those of writing, imply a working correspondence between machine and body, thus the correspondence of writing machine with writing body—in the jargon of electronic media, the interface—represents that point at which both McLuhan's "massage" and, perhaps, the laws of cybernetics become felt realities. That this interface alters human consciousness—in fact problematizes, as my qualifier would suggest, what we mean by "consciousness"—is a measure of our connectedness with other bodies, both living and nonliving. I have in fact attempted in much of what follows to work out the implications of this interface by insisting upon the metaphor of connectedness (a cultural glue—by which I do mean to point to the need for a corresponding solvent) as crucial to contemporary cybersocial experience. The salient questions of the coming century, I would argue, will have less to do with whether one will or will not choose to be connected to literal or figurative networks than with the sorts of options accessible to those who have always already been suffering (and perhaps profiting) from a variety of mis- and disconnections, external and internal. Further, the connections that electronic media most effectively foreground are those born of networking: the links between readers and writers, or, on the nets, between lurkers and posters, can be fostered by machines that *talk* with one another (and I am aware that this metaphor yet annoys many, like myself, for whom conversation is more than data transmission). This requires a truly interactive textual interface, one composed with an eye toward surprise as well as enlightenment, one that permits knowledge to grow in the direction of what is unexpected, unknown, contingent. This requires—and here my critical predisposition is perhaps most apparent—a poetics of process.[30]

Both the textual and the machine interfaces of electronic media are becoming more and more transparent largely as a consequence of user-friendly technologies,

---

30. In more explicitly ideological terms, *feminist* cyborg imagery may support, as Cynthia L. Selfe has argued, "complex articulations of possibilities and gaps, of connections and contradic-

and users are thereby tempted to forget that their mental and physical interactions—even bodily gestures—have in fact been engineered *into* the machine through a complex application of a host of sciences and technologies—cybernetics as accommodated by ergonomics, statistics, materials science, and so forth. Hence the revelation that constitutes the seductive promise, and socializing potential, of cyberspace: in offering a virtually unique experience of a virtually original simulation, it can incorporate our dreams.[31] Through a merging and consequent conflation of social technology and individual taste, the collective would thus seem to have found a way both to circumscribe and reinstate "individuality." Further, this encounter between human and machine, albeit delimited as a function of (human) life processes and machine design, provides for the apparent resurrection of bodily capabilities otherwise modified by or sacrificed to the encroachments of age, and without that shared mortality intrinsic to *inter vivos* interaction. From the standpoint of the physically disabled, an enabling utility specific to such technologies may justifiably be regarded as a godsend. Again, the double edge: one would do well to note that our social order has devised a number of successful, nonsectarian technologies, and that such technologies rarely fail in raising the spectre of

tions in current democratic political action." Cynthia L. Selfe, "Politicizing and Inhabiting Virtual Landscapes as Discursive Spaces," Rearticulating Education and the New Information Technologies, online, (conference), Internet, 15–30 Nov. 1992; quoted with permission of the author. Mark C. Taylor unpacks several of the philosophical gradients informing the figure of the cyborg in *Nots* (Chicago: U of Chicago P, 1993). His final chapter, "The Betrayal of the Body: Live Not," provides a somewhat rambling, intriguing stroll through information theory, cybernetics, cyborgs, systems, and disease, opening to some rather detailed speculation as to the human body's autoimmune response—all with an emphasis on the (linguistic and ontological) status of the "not." Finally: The essays in *Virtual Realities and Their Discontents*, ed. Robert Markley (Baltimore: Johns Hopkins UP, 1995) serve to deconstruct the implicit binaries I've been hard at work exploiting throughout this introduction (five of the six essays appeared formerly in the journal *Configurations*). Editor Markley asserts that "In one respect, the essays in this collection are dedicated to suggesting that the death of logocentrism has been greatly exaggerated" (1). Fair enough—even virtual reality requires a reality check. I would merely observe (1) that efforts to establish critical-methodological continuities and rationalities in the face of shifting media are to be applauded even as each such efforts must of necessity be subject to a (for example, materialist) critique of corresponding methodology; (2) that "the death of logocentrism has been greatly exaggerated" can in these conservative, often cynical political times constitute for some a reassurance, even a *celebration*, of prevailing logocentrisms; and (3) that however healthy a corrective to the more messianic aspects of vr, the book's surface effect (i.e., its *formal* content) once again consists of that left-to-right (wink) marginal justification that typifies the consensual hallucination of scholarly sentencing (cf. this page)—which should be taken less as critique than as recognition of the (momentary?) waning transparency of such form.

31. For a useful compendium of essays centered around the vital question of social "integration" as this relates to individual "embodiment," see Jonathan Crary and Sanford Kwinter, eds., *Incorporations* (New York: Zone, 1992).

unprecedented social need. What I regard as crucial here, in any case, is the extent to which both death and life, in conjunction with the gradual blurring of natural genres by those of the artificial, are undergoing rapid social transfiguration within a capitalist legislative edifice, and with only a modicum of concomitant public interaction.[32]

• • • •

If the challenge of electronic media is to find ways to provide for a re-membering of the body, a body that finds itself ever more frequently face-to-face with such media, my contribution in the pages that follow brings with it a final irony: despite my attempt in this introduction to suggest otherwise, the six folds of my text are themselves likely to be viewed as highly disjunctive, a disparate grouping of artificial appendages that, together, hardly comprise a coherent body of work. Stitched together out of linguistic pieces that can only approximate the living, nonliving, and dead materialities of this world as it is currently construed—and I am conscious here of *my* place in this world, my necessarily delimited and provisional sensibility as a member of a specific race, economic class, gender, profession, and nationality (among shifting others)—my Frankenstein text itself indicates the extent to which the apparent litter of culture is recyclable not simply through "organs of reality" but through the inventions of real organs, distended with blood, sweat, and tears.[33] The human fiber that threads its way through each of the following anatomies is that most elusive and variegated of commonplace constructs, love. Narcissistic, generous, sacrificial, sanctimonious, manipulative, forthcoming, ingenuous, skeptical, mercurial, enduring, implacable, easy, ethereal, earthy—love's inherent contradictions provide potential bond and certain obstacle for nurturing the emergence of vital social networks in a world marked more and more by its virtual constructions. Even to a degree greater than in Henry

---

32. Popular culture is rife with (often televised) references to genetic engineering, robotics, artificial intelligence, nanotechnology, virtual reality, and the like. Yet futuristic programming, whether software, hardware, or wetware, is in itself hardly a measure of informed interaction—a public actively grappling with the question of what it will take to establish "the relation between thought and action in social life." See Clifford Geertz, "Blurred Genres: The Refiguration of Social Thought," *Critical Theory since 1965*, eds. Hazard Adams and Leroy Searle, (Tallahassee: Florida State UP, 1986) 523. A good place to begin to examine the technological basis of such life-death controversies is the volume edited by Christopher G. Langton, *Artificial Life*, vol. 6, Santa Fe Institute, Studies in the Sciences of Complexity, Proceedings of an interdisciplinary workshop on the synthesis and simulation of living systems held Sept. 1987, in Los Alamos, New Mexico (Reading: Addison-Wesley, 1989). I am grateful to Kathleen Biddick of the Center for Cultural Studies at University of California, Santa Cruz, for drawing my attention to this volume (and subsequent such compilations).

33. Cf. Ernst Cassirer, *Language and Myth*, trans. Susanne K. Langer (New York: Dover, 1953).

Adams's day, this is an age of "physics stark mad in metaphysics," and the conflicts emerging from such everyday conceptual transgressions thrust upon social creatures—creatures of habit—may well be expected to produce alternative spaces through which to transact expression and dialogue. Hence I might lay claim to having thereby disrupted the illusion of a homogeneous and continuous conceptual space, but my work emerges less, perhaps, from a certain theoretical initiative toward the design of fragmented spatialities that engender critical peripeteia than from my having encountered and acted upon messy, fuzzy realities, realities diffused and distorted through the fluctuating rhythms of geotemporal exigency. Through a literal shaping of the symbolic new as well as the real, language connects us with our metabolic status: this is an inherently historicized, aged, and aging affair, and it makes of pasts what it will by attending to present needs and exploiting future concerns. Neither our bodies nor the world's body, in my view, should be asked to sustain the construction of global technological networks without a corresponding development of critical and creative apparatus designed to inflect such constructions with the recognition of the all-too-human and ecological imperatives at stake—unless, that is, we are willing to forgo for the most part an examination of present states of consciousness, overlook current bio- and ecopolitical controversies, and place our trust in whatever it is lies just over the horizon.[34]

---

34. It seems appropriate here to end this rather discursive proem by noting but a few of the more recent critical statements that suggest a renewed appreciation of the arts (and the artist) in forging such apparatus, even during these troubling times of NEA cutbacks and the like: Charles Bernstein, "What's Art Got to Do with It? The Status of the Subject of the Humanities in the Age of Cultural Studies," *American Literary History* Winter 1993: 597–615, and "Provisional Institutions: Alternative Presses and Poetic Innovation," MLA Convention, Royal York Hotel, Toronto, 29 Dec. 1993; Sandra Braman, "From Virtue to Vertu to the Virtual: Art in the Net," *Readerly/Writerly Texts* 3.1 (Spring/Summer 1996); Christopher Funkhouser, ed., "Toward a Literature Moving outside Itself: The Beginnings of Hypermedia Poetry," online, World Wide Web, 31 May 1996 <http:// cnsvax.albany.edu/~poetry/hyperpo.html>; Jay L. Lemke, *Textual Politics: Discourse and Social Dynamics* (London: Taylor & Francis, 1995); and Derek Owens, *Resisting Writings (and the Boundaries of Composition)* (Dallas: Southern Methodist UP, 1994). In addition, James J. Sosnoski's *Token Professionals and Master Critics: A Critique of Orthodoxy in Literary Studies* (Albany: State U of New York P, 1994) might be especially useful to artists with academic affiliation who wish to understand exactly what they are up against. I believe that the (cross-) cultural bases and biases of poetic license (latter term used advisedly) should be explored with due regard to the sorts of issues raised by Paul Gilroy in *The Black Atlantic: Modernity and Double Consciousness* (Cambridge: Harvard UP, 1993). Alternative aesthetic-critical practices will doubtless be foreclosed upon by commodity culture, as well as academic orthodoxies, without critical intervention attentive to the historical "mutation, hybridity and intermixture" associated with black-diasporic political realities; as Gilroy concludes, "The history of blacks in the West and the social movements that have affirmed and rewritten that history can provide a lesson which is not restricted to blacks " (223). Finally: I can think of no better way to highlight the shortcomings of *this* book, *this* bookend, than to refer readers to (the late) Bill Readings' *The University in Ruins* (Cambridge, MA: Harvard UP, 1996). Readings's is one of those rare books that encourages us to think past the many platitudes of the postsecondary present.

ANATOMY OF A MIND

Writing | the life and death of the mind

Edited by J. A.

19-30 July 1992

I. PRELIMINARIES

Of that
fine madness
as Drayton wrote of Marlowe
Which rightly should possess a poet's brain:

The or a poetics
of dislocation
suggests that the problem
is not in our stars
uh-uh
but in our categories:

As certain preconceptual structuring intersects
with certain social structuring
at the individual human interface
the organism is assigned another category
{Phenotype}
collapsing into what could
only two decades back
yet be described as
the wallpapered materialities of space and time
varying with the threshold of circumstance.

Forget ethos for a moment, retain
if you please
the possibility of loss:
an embodiment is not, properly
an ecology made solely of one's mind but
out of a biological many, intrinsically demo-
graphic.

Many minds, linkedtooneanotherlinked
togethertoandonadriftingplanetmapped
however culturally or
or ideologically or   as State(s) of or
or informationally . . .
Ahhhh——in   formationally——

——it all sounds mighty cerebral, no?
noetic and now
once upon a time
a brain trust having stormed across
washing the old territories, the old

imperatives and these days, the articulation
altered this way
or that
affords no story
architectural, archaeological, or otherwise
to support
high-mindedness . . .

And in the meantime...

paper to pixel
materiality to materialization
but lo   and behold
whether connectionist paradigm
["The term 'connectionist' is, in general, applied both to spreading-activation and PDP models. The more
recent term, "neural nets" usually refers to PDP and true neural models" (Dell and Juliano 2).—Ed.]
or among endless simulations
some argue
rather neopragmatically
for——not "mere" metaphors
but *models*
and here is all
the difference:

mind, brained
often justifiably
by the Churchlands, Minsky, Dennett
shards of cybernetic consciousness strewn hither and thither
and what is left is, yes, explained
away
allowing for an alternative
generic mind, possibl-y preprogrammed
or
upon entering
NATURE'S BACK DOOR
is asserted
a self-organizing complexity
dynamic continuous nested evolutionary blah blah blah
in so many ways
let's say
reflexively a self in flux a
fragmentary whole
as James might have put it and what is perhaps more
over/determined
even where one hangs

one's hat
nor by will
nor imagination
for what, truly, are these?
but by social construction on the one hand
and natural construction on the other
hard soft wet or
plastic
two discursive categories
and what would a non-discursive category be, anyhow?
&
here's the catch
the monkey's in the middle
internal externalized
through countless research claims
e.g., "Yes, we who construct
construct both realities similarly
inside to
and from outside
and so we who construct
are yet constructed
in accordance
with the dictates
of natural and social processing
as we come to know
i.e., construct
same . . . "
our construct/ion\s hence
become laws, jus scriptum
& non scriptum
and mind
becoming
residual in all of this
a consequence of specific neural
uses and
as such
potentially retrofitted
by attention to
as Turner tells it, as the cognitive rhetoricians would have it
its defaults
that is
until suitable silicon circuitry is available . . .

Some things gotta go, but
a mind
as most Americans are surely well
aware
is a terrible thing
to waste.

> "Is a recycling of mind still
> in the cyberspatial cards?
> And might electronic correspondence
> correspond to the displacement of global defaults?"

Tentatively, and note the line
breaks:

> It is not yet clear whether we will see a turn
> back toward the heritage of cybernetics
> or simply a "massively parallel" variant of current cognitive theory and
> symbol-processing design.
> Although the
> new connectionism
> may breathe
> new life
> into
> cognitive modeling research,
> it suffers an uneasy balance between symbolic and physiological description. Its
> spirit
> harks back to the cybernetic
> concern with real biological systems,
> but the detailed
> models
> typically assume a simplistic
> representational
> base much closer to traditional artificial intelligence. Connectionism, like its parent
> cognitive theory,
> must be placed in the
> category
> of brash unproved
> hypotheses,
> which have not really begun to deal with the complexities of mind
> and whose current explanatory power is extremely limited.

Winograd 216

A plai e, then, for this this dis
locatiᵒn:

Post   hum
or   o us
ly dis concerted, like any good per
former   [more later...
and punning madly
mind begins
by reflecting upon the local sites
of past articulations, cut-and-pasted
constructions
incl. maybe a refrain or two
from childhood. It thinks
or consists of thought
thought emerging from its failure
to grasp consciousness
for all that it can be
is . . .

Language speaks its turn
but method
so readily become Policy
mind searches, impolitely
in prototypically Romantic fashion
for partial insight
into the
ineffable
nature
of its death.

[Note that at least one observer, Paulo Freire (the Younger), while commenting on
Kenneth Burke's discussion of "poetry and illusion" (Burke 198 ff.), remarks that we
may well be living in a "golden age of comedy," and that humor is therefore "most
assuredly in jeopardy." He cites as examples, among numerous others, the prevalence
of cable tv comedy programming as well as the issuing of (U. S. Postal Service)
"Comedians" stamps. See Freire 514. It is likewise pertinent to observe the
irrelevance of Russian Formalism to this line of inquiry.—Ed.]

II. MIND TO BRAIN

Both go back a long way together, even as
words. Grammar acts as though it were a
minor character, but we know better. The
protagonist examines its narrative liabilities:
there would appear to be no way out, and
clearly brain death requires a spiritual or
lyrical turn, premature at this point in the
investigation. Symbolization: all lexica
bespeak the shifting lexia that comprise
intentionality, an inventory designed to cap-
ture what at its root stems as much from
amorphous, haphazard logic as from the
experiential constraints of matter and
energy, flesh and blood. The beauty of it in
the convergence of harmonic irregularities
and dissonant rhythms, waveforms of
thought and feeling that elide or recrudesce
only to multiply the possibilities of particle
and pattern, sensation and memory. A
plasma, perpetually nascent, this thing in
time, this finite process, a living and lived
abstraction this life of the mind erupting
amid those grey and glaciated domains of
the social that extend throughout invention
and beyond to disclose that which trickles to
and fro, casually or passionately, at the
perimeters. And consonant with this chaos
of timing, a sensed yet inarticulable ripeness
that underwrites all modes of structuration
and order, without and within, rendering
the mind's own space in time somehow
illegible, a purposive phasing motioning
ever toward its own cessation even as it provides the content prerequisite to growth,
awareness, discovery, writing, transformation, speaking, acting, exchanging . . .

The sound of rain is familiar and reassuring. It appears to repeat itself. The sound of rain. Repeat itself. It appears to. To it is familiar and reassuring. To it is the sound. To it reassures. The rain. Resounds. To rain. To its sound. Repeat.

Take 1:

In a world of images, has the life of the mind become no more and no less than the life of the image? This opens to a revaluation of what it means to be an intellectual, academic or otherwise.

Is mind simply one of various extensions of brain, a working concept, a means to an end, a technology, hence compatible with all such technologies? This opens to a revaluation of what it means to be human, inhuman or otherwise.

Is the passing of mind as a working concept—or, at the very least, the wholesale abandonment of more humanistic notions of mind—one indication that life itself is to be rethought, demystified, reduced, or supplemented? This opens to a revaluation of what it means to be alive, non-living or otherwise.

Take 1 x 2:

The mind has receded in context. The reasons are politically informed, expedient. Other questions persist. E.g.: What is the nature of mind such that it is capable of investigating its own   artifice artificiality instrumentality by placing out of sight its raison d'être—the dualism from which it has arisen, that of mind and brain\body—in order to yield a better approximation of its status as a topos, a place, both subject and object of its self-examination?

Take 2:

The media with and against which such analysis is formulated, wrought, articulated, are likewise extensions of humankind, hence mind has become for brain\body a see-through mediator of media.   And   in   seeing   through, brain\body has seen past. As though content were a function of formal distillation, a uniformity inhering across different versions of the same text. As though diversity revealed a common core of value, eth(n)ically. OR is it that we of habit and need desire things so? To gloss Bernstein after Barthes and Bataille writes of the erotic nature of poetics, the escape into that (ab)usage whose violence and pleasure we at once resist, are nauseated by, succumb to, and learn from? So this, then, is the printed copy—and we suppose the hypertext to have already been composed, somewhere upstairs.   What follows next? Does a new, or no longer useful, relationship between mind and brain somehow correspond to the advent of pixels? Do non-volatile memory storage and instantaneous character deletion guage à rearticulation of articulation? Perhaps we have reached a state of KNOW-ING such that we require the development of an evolutionary, revised organ of consciousness, measurable as an epiphenomenon of broader cultural and biotechnological trends, an intelligence that understands its provisional basis in the global scheme of information processing—in cyberorganismic terms, cognition.

Take 3:

But what of recognition? One more time: this is your brain on drugs?[1] The history of the avant garde, of experimental art, reveals an inversion of the dictates of experimentalism: what is congenial to verification through repetition comes to be regarded as culturally inert, socially suspect aes-thet-i-cal-ly inferior. Readymades, automatic writing, action painting, free jazz, language poetry: ways to induce an active response to manufactured sculpture, painting, music, language. Electronic media are immanently iterative, replicative, hence the pathways they provide are fraught with postindustrial motives. (All of this has been written in another place, offered to another network, and plagiarized even there.) Yet it is through these selfsame media—through the screen, hence invariably, at some locus of social points, rec'd cinematographically—that mind has come to revise, resee, revisit itself—to repeat, again and again, and potentially to see through and past the ontology of repetition, habit. But social circuits have developed shortcuts to cross even cosmic wiring, and the postmodern fix has fixed it so that only a precisely manufactured, Hollywoodized mind can afford to escape, to lose itself. But where? And is this not the brain speaking?

---

1. Cf., by contrast, Edward Dorn's *Gunslinger*: "Time is more fundamental than space./It is, indeed, the most pervasive/of all the categories/in other words/theres plenty of it" (5).

Repeat. To its sound. To rain. Resounds.
The rain. To it reassures. To it is the
sound. To it is familiar and reassuring. It
appears to. Repeat itself. The sound of
rain. It appears to repeat itself. The
sound of rain is familiar and reassuring.

III. BRAIN TO MIND

Here by lifting from   others
coextensively
and working through
remorse . . .

Brain\body the new body
wrap, the smart machine
fast
the easy way
like radio like topic
sentences like
no deposit no like
return   like is li
ke si_____d like ... ————   ———

and what of res is tance?
To?

3 favorite books:

What is attention? In one point of view, the essential effect of attention is to render
perception more intense and to spread out its details; regarded in its *content*, it
would resolve itself into a certain magnifying of the intellectual state. But, on the
other hand, consciousness testifies to an irreducible difference of form between this
increase of intensity and that which is owing to a higher power of the external stimu-
lus: it seems indeed to come from within and to indicate a certain attitude adopted
by the intellect. But it is here that the difficulty begins, for the idea of an intellectual
attitude is not a clear idea. . . . Stage by stage we shall be led on to define attention as
an adaptation of the body rather than of the mind and to see in this attitude of
consciousness mainly the consciousness of an attitude.

                                                                                    Bergson 100

It is his body that is his answer, his body intact and fought for, the absolute of his
organism in its simplest terms, this structure evolved by nature, repeated in each act
of birth, the animal man. . . . In this intricate structure are we based, now more
certainly than ever (besieged, overthrown), for its power is bone muscle nerve blood
brain   a man, its fragile mortal force its old eternity, resistance.

                                                                                    Olson 13-14

Today, however, the inner logic of research in cognitive psychology, linguistics, neuroscience, artificial intelligence, evolutionary theory, and immunology seems to incorporate more and more working elements of an enactive orientation. . . . We have now reached the end of our presentation of the enactive approach in cognitive science. We have seen not only that cognition is embodied action, and so inextricably tied to histories that are lived, but also that these lived histories are the result of evolution as natural drift. Thus our human embodiment and the world that is enacted by our history of coupling reflect only one of many possible evolutionary pathways. We are always constrained by the path we have laid down, but there is no ultimate ground to prescribe the steps that we take. It is precisely this lack of an ultimate ground that we have evoked at various points in this book by writing of groundlessness. This groundlessness of laying down a path is the key philosophical issue that remains to be addressed.

Varela, Thompson, and Rosch 213-14

Plus a tune, of sorts:

I wish my life was a non-stop Hollywood movie show,
A fantasy world of celluloid villains and heroes,
Because celluloid heroes never feel any pain
And celluloid heroes never really die.

The Kinks

Co mentary

write-along
not of explication

but of choice

a tool requires

than a tool, more

a line   to plumb

and in tending toward
        the form reveals itself
            a series of questions?
                having been asked before?
                    or displaced a bit?
                        and dis contented, each stroke
                            each stroke, each absence
                                a world of meaning
                                    dislocated, and the mind

frets
f or the body
sought
in the body
of text
with each
new phrase a
parse
of electrochemical
dependency
triggering learned
or learned
responses
capturing the data
live
this brain
draining
exhausts only
the possibility
of local nourishment
for the moment
the f orm
     reveals itself
        a series of questions?
           or displaced a bit?
          as before?
                  tomorrow and
tomorrow and

                         is another
day and
in which
to round up
the usual
suspects . . .

Usually
the contours

the surfaces
of memory
linger, int
er
act, but (t)her
e
a single sign
obscuring
all that is not
literature
they flicker
w/o a trace
of remorse:

A.series.of.reflexive
dilemmas.........brain
gradually....merging
with.......its.........own
formless...content.a.
.filler.for..symmetry

To see
& not to see
through the screen
A &
not A . . .

If energized hardware ='d brain
& software ='d mind
& if the analogs emerged
& now collapse into
the metaphor that murders
pineapples . . .

The thing is
not a text yet
to know
it
as a thing-
text is perhaps   ufficient . . .

Not a rhetoric of mind
but of brain
but of brain.brain

the technology, the construct/ion
the mind's I   witness
not——

—>   Consciousness of an attitude
adapted by the body
toward mortality
grounded solely
in a particular time
corresponding to
a particular (i.e., (o)lived) plot:

Attending to the form of each plot, episode, duration, span
is a matter of attitude, content
magnified, yes   quantities-cum-qualities[2]
and acted upon to yield
content still
formed, altering with
such renewed content im plies grow th, a biograph, an auto
mobile ≠ to = to ≠ to . . . .   endgame,

the form and substance of each life's
end er and what of *this* place   [As in "He's chewing the scenery."—Ed.]
vis-à-vis that, what
of the keys to
the alphabet, these
perfected moments
of space?

                            Shadows, you say?

To motion forth
and back
between the words
the places memories
the concepts signs
the thoughts things
the images   of things   & i n an ag e of im ag ing ban ks
feelings:

To recall
what must be

---

2. Cf. Plato.

the catastrophe of, that unites even
two
words concepts signs things
people:

To reconcile only
a need
for cross
talk crazy
at times sophomoric
or silly
as is
is necessary:

The faiths and figures we 1st. person pl. pronouns employ
to figure the hungers[3] longings

       hunger

it's a sub-urban rhythm/plays itself out
even in this country/but a voice calls to me
against chant of insect/my retreat
against hoarse murmur/of bullfrog
my citied white hide/against night descending
quick as a black eye/a car
comes throbbing back/slams the breaks
a voice calls to me/Get in

I gotta go/don't know
what it is/don't wanna

After a while we stop/I tap the driver
on the shoulder/hand her a five-spot
am greeted by the light/of day three faces
woman man child/mother father son
a lover/I once knew holds my arm
we're downtown/somewhere
somewhere/in the street

woman/please sir we're hungry
man/holding child atop shoulder
we just want food/woman
we don't want no money sir/just food please
food sir just food/for our baby

---

3. Cf. the self-consuming artifacts of George A. Romero's zombie trilogy.

44

familiar lines/tearing through
and around each/gestures screaming for
pride choking eyes taut/from need three lined
even the child's lovely/three
yes yes black/folk begging
begging for/food
a family/begging
woman mother father/husband child son
as any family/they was & were folk
crossing the lines/of color
in the street/for food
in the face of/their faces
like mine/my lover's ours
of pain/of this country
of people/ like any other
of terra firma/familiar
but for the grace of ...

                       Let's face it—'we' can't *consume* this stuff
      we all gotta go . . . *together? at once? leerically?* . . . and who is it   cares?
                                    hungers longings this time
       study of a writer's writing—whiteness *is* atissue, the bodies at stake black &
              white, homeless to know 'we' ground ourselves in what 'we' exact
                 from others & but to exact only a grammared presence of earthly
                     otherness by way of ensuring a 'we' each of equal measure
                         to speak one's own mind—dialectically & no, & how
with ten or less
fingers
for five these
techniques that is in sum, these careless lines to their margins unjust
having brought one or two to a man or a
woman or a
child, black, a (-)typed imagery, story   survive amid unfed poverties of
w & b, only to the verge of   2+ technologies
and while it may be true
that $2+ \geq 1$
it remains to be demonstrated   [w/o recourse to (de)segregated suffering?—Ed.]
whether collaboration or communication across a new set of constraints
will ensure that the the the   fresher symptoms of the times
disempower brainless or mindless actions or
both, "'native' 'intelligence'" (viz., cough) notwithstanding:

                                      Simply to take it as a fiat
                                  that change brings about
                                   change is like asking
                                  for a penny's worth
                                        etc.

45

these pages are numbered, The numbering of
sure as our hours
sure as   as   alas! to cook, baby, w/o short ning

[This alludes to the so-called "sin of emission."—Ed.]

and not to count
digitally
only to refuse, is but
what's going on outside
and inside you, what's
could be
s
getting more and more
fuse
inute
by
e . . .

w/o, at and in tending to
things have gotten   a complex
as the signs that mind is, its text
and all that contributes
and an original insight, ex post   facto   nor pretending to know whence
travels around, here and there
may be w/o a plan
that explains the place
w/o intending to ... another book appropriation then
again first person
by a third man:

By "intention" I mean here what uses a sign in a thought. The intention seems to interpret,
to give the final interpretation; which is not a further sign or picture, but something else—
the thing that cannot be further interpreted. But what we have reached is a psychological,
not a logical terminus.

Wittgenstein 42e

So go ahead
just wish it so:

[It might be wise to jot down a thing or two here
about the non-economic aspects of an
impoverished mind, but just imagine
how much sweeter
a strawberry smells
when you've gone w/o for a while.]

          "In the end
           of print
      is its new beginning
           tasty
          as hell
        a paradise
      for synthesizing
       odds 'n ends
      even southpaws
      and institutions
   predicated on economic
       independence
        will falter
       to the extent
      that they restrict
        the flow of
      transgressions . . .

"O.k.—so there IS money to be made out of all of this
          speculation
      but the greatest pleasure
        may well be restricted
          to the smallest
            number."

          (Simple beep.)

                                    Er ors
                               as deviation
                              from standard
                                 deviation
                             presume upon
                          what is correct and
                         but what is thought?
                              to be correct
                         about word production

reproduces
but what is thought?
to be correct
about thinking:

Note how passive
acceptance
marks
the question:
mind
by all accounts
THE telos of model
due in no small measure
to common research apparatus
but a model of word production
reproduces not simply words or
thoughts but the constraints
distributed throughout
the network culture
hastens toward.

And these shape, determining
minds and mind dis
assembling categories
surprise   surprise
in public view
shape public spaces, too   the practices   speeches & scrawls of
insides & outs   a s he arts.

Is it, then
and to force the momento, decidedly awkwardly
to its crisis, that the death of print

[This reference to print's "death" points to the apparent assumption of its
passing primacy as a communications technology.—Ed.]

permits the death of mind, or
more constructively, of mind's
life? Hence life
and death anew, new
limits
to come, at last
under (consumer) re
view?

•   The essential power to neglect the fact that writing would have life for support, finds itself facilitated and theoretically justified by the resource of books. Books seem to be there to preserve writing and to allow it to constitute itself in its own space, separate and as if separated from any life. Writing, forced to give itself as the expression or affirmation of life, has never satisfied either writing or life. The refined categories, those of existence, the play of being and of time, offered to the question of writing, have been able to serve to keep such a question "alive," but without giving us any illusion about this "borrowed" life. Life contests writing that conceals itself from life or reduces it. But the contest comes from writing that leaves plenitude to life and unexceptionable presence to the Living, bearer of life, while writing can certainly propose itself as that which would exhaust life in order to inscribe itself at the limit of life; finally the proposition makes room for this other, completely other: writing only writes itself at the limit of writing, there where the book, although still there, is the pressure of the end (without end) of books.

Blanchot 56-57

Tempting to read this
book end
as what we have had
in mind
but a self-avowed, meditative
fragment
must be handled
delicately, she sez:

> It is in the observation that writing's claim to, on life
> (note the b
> latant personification), its claim to wholeness
> givenness
> is obscured, hence preserved
> by the preservative qualities of books:
> Take away books, substitute the stubborn ephemera, say
> aloud for a change
> of contemporary writing technologies
> and writing's claim
> as independent lifeform
> might be made
> to appear that much more tenuous, inter if you will
> vivos-ly:

But writing yet writes
this other, completely other
comprising the recognition
a challenge to Life
that all writing is written finally
as though it were not   written
finally
        as though as death
it could situate its referential
or experiential absence
in the present   writing
        and read as though
it does not merely and profoundly repeat that
which could never have been written

now   as though this   now
were the space of its identity its   appeal
to presence inspiring   authorizing
a transgression against   against
that limit preserved
by the apparent end (w/o end?)
of books but a transgression   that
which can only be writing this
in the face of   the dead space of
death and thus is in actuality
is   unknowable unthinkable unwritable
never to be
unwritten unvoiced   yet even in a living tongue
unlivable . . .

[Evidence of a brogue here might have been persuasive. Or
the word "noggin."—Ed.]

Familiar fine-tuning? And IF a provisional book end-------

communicating or collaborating FTF in real
time is one thing permitting readers more dialectical options
is one thing writing or reading as though
one lives through such activity as though
such activity brings one that much closer
to life a/

        synchronously
and death
is one thing but to forget or   recall
that writing IS writing
written as though it were capable
of inscribing itself at the limit of life
not out of an appeal to wholeness
but out of a denial of its after-ness its meanings
to an ending or
TECHNOLOGY?.............   (is another thing etc.)

& the end of (e) s   p   ace frankly
             no   w   here in   site............

To displace defers   but to dislocate   think/write gene
rations of   queue bists
      re places   relo cates res to res to writing
its mind   to life
its writing.............And maybe that's a thing more
to think about.[4]

NB   *M*   *ustn't forget how*   *to*
sinlaughin   *gboogie*   *w*   *rite*   *mus*
blasgramorphoneming   *(faxtaxsaxvaxmaxwax)* *e.g., sur* l *e vi* l *l iv e* l *rus*
                                           t   *nt*
                                 forege t h   *ow to*
          sh   *ake*   *o*   *ur*   *as sesha*   *nds*
                                                  up
        an ddown   *modulat in g moveth*   *e*   *st and up*
    ard   *s*   *the prop ertie s,f air* *ly th*   *es e*
                                                 rea l   *s*
Z!POP!mmmmmmmmmmmmmmmmmmmmmmmmmmmmmm...

---

4. Gertrude Stein might help here, but, like love and landing a job, some other time.

CODICIL

All
or n   one
by way of struggling
to suggest
                  & to suggest is itself to be in conflict with one's own? motives

that, more visibly
the content
&, less visibly
the form(-content)
of electronic media
though differing from this stuff
in clearly demonstrable ways   albeit bound to be a resemblance
are in no way guarantors   like it & no
of a mind
or subject
or terminal looming on the cybernetic horizon
capable of self-CONTROL
(though new such minds may surely so loom . . .)

that a modified mind
is decidedly in the cards
an assertion to be evaluated   like most postulates
independently of how one
shuffles the deck, &
in the midst of social ferment
if by "social" is meant
something like
a group of folks who drink beer together every
other Wednesday night; further

that ALL the stacks
may be loaded
beyond our wildest
suppositions, thresholds, again
distending out, paths paved with &
into what we may b-b-become; specifically

that mind itself

as a working concept
is jeopardized
probably owing to the global implementation
of a Host of orthodox, late print-age beliefs\techniques
via software magic etc.
& the coeval development of increasingly powerful
& efficient information systems
personal & otherwise; hence

that it follows, reasonably   by nor from
design
the reasons having much to do
theoretically
with how
language
environment
& the interrelations of
genetically similar
readers & writers
boys & girls
        each speaking
        & writing
        & understanding
        a different language
provide the basis for the construction
of mutable categories
useful
& otherwise

that poetrics a hybrid
esp. for poets   what can never be ALL   bUSinEss
provides a rhetoric, has all along
for interrogating, indicting language practices re   creations
incl. rhetoric
as an activity process engagement   the short & the long   of   it
                                         & certainly not forever
& ever   as a technology
underwritten/ing, as might be expected
(by) various institutions $$$ means
meanings
& for determining the value(s)   significance(s)
of in forging vital social strata   for those so de   signed

dislocating what we might like to be   to   be   person a lly
& how
mind consciousness brain body   all
to places, categories yet
undefined   unruly   (do we understand each/other?)
regions

bit by blasted, fucking bit.

[In his recently published memoirs, *Etesian Wells*, M. BOURGOIN reports being brought before the authorities for having drained his (fried) chicken on a ream of 100% cotton bond.—Ed.]

Ingredients: Charles Bernstein, *A Poetics* (Harvard UP, 1992); Henri Bergson, *Matter and Memory*, trans. N. M. Paul and W. S. Palmer (Zone Books, 1991; originally published 1896); Robin Blaser, "The Practice of Outside," in Jack Spicer, *The Collected Books of Jack Spicer* (Black Sparrow Press, 1975); Maurice Blanchot, *The Step Not Beyond* (Translation of *Le Pas Au-Dela*), trans. Lycette Nelson (State University of New York Press, 1992; originally published 1973); Toni Morrison, *Playing in the Dark: Whiteness and the Literary Imagination* (Vintage, 1992); Ludwig Wittgenstein, *Zettel*, G. E. M. Anscombe and G. H. von Wright, eds., trans. G. E. M. Anscombe (University of California Press, 1970); Edward Dorn, *Gunslinger* (Duke UP, 1989; originally published 1968); Daniel C. Dennett, *The Intentional Stance* (MIT Press, 1989); Gary S. Dell and Cornell Juliano, *Connectionist Approaches to the Production of Words,* Cognitive Science Technical Report CS-91-05 (Beckman Institute, University of Illinois at Urbana-Champaign, Feb. 1991); Terry Winograd, "Thinking Machines: Can There Be? Are We?," in James J. Sheehan and Morton Sosna, eds., *The Boundaries of Humanity: Humans, Animals, Machines* (University of California Press, 1991); Francisco J. Varela, Evan Thompson, and Eleanor Rosch, *The Embodied Mind: Cognitive Science and Human Experience* (MIT Press, 1991); Ntozake Shange, *The Love Space Demands (a continuing saga)* (St. Martin's Press, 1991); Van Halen music video, *Right Now (*song in *For Unlawful Carnal Knowledge*, Warner Bros. CD); Mark Turner, *Reading Minds: The Study of English in the Age of Cognitive Science* (Princeton UP, 1991); W. J. M. Levelt, *Speaking: From Intention to Articulation* (MIT Press, 1989); Charles Olson, "The Resistance," in Robert Creeley, ed., *Selected Writings of Charles Olson* (New Directions, 1966); Kenneth Burke, *Counter-Statement* (University of California Press, 1968; originally published 1931); Gail E. Hawisher and Cynthia L. Selfe, eds., *Evolving Perspectives on Computers and Composition Studies: Questions for the 1990s* (NCTE, 1991); The Kinks, "Celluloid Heroes," in *Everybody's In Show-Biz* (Rhino CD); Paulo Freire (the Younger), *Pedagogy of the Unimpressed*, trans. Pat Housebreak Dill (Routledge, 1991); calcium proprionate (to preserve freshness).

ANATOMY OF A SOUL

For and Against Virtual Space: The Anxieties of Writing in Real Times

14 December 1992

II

letters lurk at the perimeter		k
work is one way	i	
and if you don't know who i am is		g
there are no numbers	g	
animals come in all shapes and sizes		l
a blue glow	e	
girl runs away from		y
cucumber woman	j	
make it code red		a
acid rock and old english	r	
or is it the same way		z
here and there	b	
and if you don't know what I mean is		m
truly tired images	x	
fingers nimble		o
nibble	i	
toward the end		n
a bit of thread	f	
spools out over		u
the seas	c	
are no longer green		q
if they could	a	
to make links so		u

III

then you shall k

want to make it lean t

she told this one to me z

the fourth of every month e

the terminal is terminal said w

letters kill o

eat burnt amp toast f

said we pray x

the fourth of every month he r

said we write h

and print it out c

said to me s

this s

at ginger nibble i

on oceanic spools m

the classroom is full j

the stage is ready h

a woman runs away p

a blue glow d

toward the end l

besides a smart machine b

the terminal w

with acid rock t

playing in the background   k

a few kids and animals   y

turning of and on and then   d

and then another is left   v

waiting to see that   e

letters lurk at the perimeter   e

this represents the gist of a dream i had recently, about the letters i've only begun to understand for what they were. a fraction of existence is all it takes. the screen is a metaphor for distance. it screens anxieties wrought of separation from and reproduction by the dominant apparatus. mr. and mrs. gutenberg have left town, and taken their children with them. nobody knows whether they'll be back, nobody knows who we are, hence nobody cares what we write, including us. there is little i can do to allay my own fears, let alone yours. why we must let go is less important than why we must go on, waiting. some would kill for such knowledge. me, i'm too busy worrying about the letters, where they came from, who they belong to, who will own them next, what plot they will participate in, whether they will be here when i return. stand aside and let me write. there is nothing left to print

and if you don't who i am is

and another is left

but waiting for what? a hitchcock cameo? a local bowling legend's perfect game? that's just it. this is how they will come, this is how death leaves us behind. proximity is the measure of all things. anonymity is efficient. it marginalizes lines of influence and effluence, converting difference into familiarity. what do you say? let us sing, in graffiti. later, we will find a place to dance, together, but for now, let us sing, in steely graffiti

letters kill

letters lurk at the perimeter

and if you don't know what i mean is

ambiguity emerges from complex knowledges. how is not the point. the point is that ambiguity is clearly a useful subset of experience. it keeps you guessing, it makes me powerful, unreadable, appealing. until you lose interest, in which event i feign clarity and sublimate into a noble gas and ambiguity is inviolable. the lesson comes in avoiding too much reading too much. too much reading too much is like too much eating too much. we all know of the liabilities associated with an obese brain. even if it's a horror story, there is nothing left to print

and another is left

waiting and

it's high noon. they've arrived, and all know C inside and out. time to book, even the ventriloquist's dummy

don't worry

i'm close behind

we'll leave and be here when they get back and when they do

we have determined how to repackage ourselves for digital consumption. but we lack the means to mythologize the end product. this is because we have perfected the means and there is no end product. what's missing, in any case, is a ballad of repackaging. let us sing, then, in graffiti. let us pray. let us weep. let us laugh. let us shit our guts out and sell them for upgrades. we can afford it, can't we? i was being sincere. we have lost a generation or more to clinical cynicism, and now we look to letters at the perimeter for salvation. but scrap is scrap, rerun is rerun, draft is draft, classic is classic

a ballad of repackaging[1]

> digits in the ether/digits here and there
> our digits do the talking nearly/everywhere
> as we abhor a vacuum/we learn to live a dare
> once out of nature/is a twice-told affair
>
> Artificial as intelligence, a sentence
> shimmers across my screen, summoning me
> like a token of thanks from ages hence and
> I know I'm out of time, or seem to be.
>
> It's come down to this, then: I could sing
> to you of what will happen, has happened
> is happening between us, but you, from what
> you write, would likely take my words alone to heart.

---

[1]See Appendix A.

VI

And this is wrong, my dear, for the art
was ever in posting through humdrum matter
replying to avoid a material void, to seek in words
the solace of an earthy never-never.

(Refrain)

Unpopular though the sentiment may be
and even as they chart the drifting of a planet
words alone do not dictate realities: with them
we hack our way into the soul of a moment.

I'm no romantic, know of no lofty path
and waxing post-whatever to shield me from the heat
long now to give to you but the absence words permit
a few perishable pixels, then, to share.

So unpack your baggage, I've come to set the record
straight: this element we cohabit is both newly formed
and old—the ancients dreamt of shadows, virtual
and embodied, worded in an inkless mold.

(Refrain)

letters kill

the classroom is full

let us give up trying to pretend trying to give up pretending we are someplace
else. we are not someplace else. yet. we have made love thus far only under
a paper moon, yet we seek what is virtually meaningful and really virtual.
the sun has set, long live the sun. that you may find this fact seriously weird
means that you have lost your sense of humor. meaning that you
understand more than you should. meaning that you haven't learned
enough to teach those who haven't learned to learn

a few kids

turning of and on and then
waiting to see

and we hand them paper and pencil and pretend that they know what to do?
or a keyboard and mouse? what's the difference? with or without hands?
their bodies, like ours, seem to migrate peacefully toward a complete absence
of responsibility. where is this motion headed? this land is your land, this
land is my land, but who owns it? is growth a series of discrete

transformations? does the circuit allow for incoherence, and does it resist any
but progressive approximations of the real? and listening to the gamut
of body warmth behind
hands moist there
raise a leg this way
a bit of hair
lip curves up
almost asleep
back of knee
shifting onto stomach
perspires against thigh
engorging this
insides again
a slight murmur
palm squeezes through
crease at base
protruding ache
soft center fringed
back of ear whispers
calf quiver rising
lower back smoothly
hanging touches down
and around the side
someone who knows

and this someone who knows—who is it? somebody we know? look to the

screen: we will compose books of email exchanges, and call them books. look

to the screen: we will have sex with one another virtually, and call it sex.

look to the screen: we will try to render things a bit more democratic, and call

it a noble failure. look to the screen: invest your money wisely. believe that

tomorrow the sun will set as it has today. believe that hydrogen is the most

abundant element in the universe. believe in pain. read that curious book of

the bible that begins with e and try to determine if irony is the answer to all

our woes i am being sincere i want something to change but i can't write
down what is it what it is

here and there

look to the screen: look in the mirror: look into the eyes of someone you
love. what is it you find there of any value? t her e i sno thin glef ttopr in t

we are becoming other than ourselves

you and me, this and that

perhaps this is the chief lesson to take with us into the next millenium:
apprehension a species-level concern. and marketing letters that kill we will
recreate ourselves. numbers simply the universal code of transmission.
meaning will once again function in medieval terms and the word will give
way to a monetary icon, coin of the realm. and is there is nothing left

besides a smart machine

what is it you find there of any value? consciousness is a beautiful dodo bird.
just wait and say "see? I told you so." time to boogie
toward the end

lots of time, take it easy. i work on a time & material basis.[2] time is space,
space is material, time is material. money is money. money is access. access
is time, time is space, access is space, access is material. money conversion
negotiation currency energy spirit. money is material energy. money buys
spacetime. spirit saves money saves money buys energyless information

a few kids and animals and
letters kill

networks. money is a categorical imperative. money is mind. money is a
way and

work is one way

but what sort of way? monied ethic. monied ethos. monied all. monied
one. monied poverty

at ginger nibble
eat burnt amp toast

---

[2]See Appendix B.

now that we've left that place behind, the mere mention of. i won't let it happen again, i promise. education is what we want in order to know. computers and literacy: questions revolving around our basic insecurities when faced with intelligence emanating from without. programming knowledge passes for insider's information, but has it become holier than thou? why not resist? and why resist? and why not question our insecurities? securities? nobody does this for a living. money

eat burnt amp toast

o.k. let's articulate a plan, from elsewhere: "the learner enjoys learning and is actively involved"; "new knowledge is viewed as relevant and is connected to previous experience"; "basic skills are integrated with the thinking process"; "opportunities exist to go deeply into the subject matter"; "opportunities exist to practice and get feedback"; "teams solve problems that have multiple solutions." notice the position of quotation marks—before the semicolon. this from the company that designs makes markets cpu chips for my macintosh. this the land of opportunity. ther eisn oth ingl efttop rint

make it code red

ready? they are looking over my shoulder even now, without timbuktu. even now, despite the traffic, someone has documented that i had a stubborn urinary tract infection late last year. i admitted it, of course, i confessed to someone who knows, an agent, not a "'change agent' in education" (as above) but an agent nonthlss. this is hostile territory. i am no longer mobile—thank you, pete townshend & co. where did I leave my laptop? one's medical history is so utterly impersonal, care   ful

there is a time for every season, and it's that time again: time to drop a few names, before i lose you: foucault hughes deleuze drucker drexler treichler joris byrd stone olson tal ficus rex agre moulthrop whitman kaplan kelly [...] miekal and liz was fuchs joyce eyal ulmer guattari luigi-bob spicer yurik petry laurel rosenberg blitz coleridge baudrillard crump porush mallarmé lyotard levi monk prince fowler fox-good unsworth levy owens kant hawisher serres poster north van pelt sam-i-am nous refuse art linkletter. make up your own lisp, if you like. or you can use mine, though some of the names might object

the stage is ready

we're almost there here. we're almost to the point at which certain questions, whether answered or no, will no longer be asked. this is the way of the screen, and all our yesterdays have lighted fools the way to. tomorrow is tomorrow is tomorrow. students want to get on with it, get it on. so what do you say—let's? like us, assuming we is not them, they are subjected to disease, crime, poverty, bureaucracy, statistics, aging. they may not know it, but they need instruction in institutional survival. if we can know no better, we yet know this: there are no rules for once and for all

i know: keeping in mind that the social ideological historical political and cosmic ramifications may be left somewhat dangling, this is our domain, not theirs. help to let them let go, a present absence attending. we'll be there to wave goodbye, in any case, p(aper)articles in hand, rife with conventions. a bit of beauty i keep coming back to: a kiss to build a dream on, w/no chaste paper tissue ersatz connective issue, all evidence is doctored. t he reis not hingle fttoprin tt here is nothing left to print

our lives are recursive. some times we can help but move on. in *exactly* the same way, sort of. the line we all believe, it's so true

stay close—time to dance
our way out of this dialectical joint
but first
a quick reality check
to ensure that my pedagogy
is working properly:

POP QUIZ

INSTRUCTIONS: Match the items on the right (or left) with the corresponding items on the left (or right) by writing the appropriate letter in the space provided.

Argument *FOR*	Corollary *AGAINST*
A. virtual communities	__no(i)sy neighbors
B. instant account balances	__life on borrowed times
C. computer literacies	__human illiteracies
D. decentralized workplace	__bring it on home
E. ecological enlightenment	__network conspiracies
F. flexible work hours	__sexual frustration (i.e., virtually)
G. gothic database	__gothic database
H. home economics	__child labor
I. income enhancement	__tax evasion
J. distributed access	__joe code
K. kellogg's rice crispies	__snap crackle pop
L. distance learning	__retraining
M. machine precision	__machine prejudice
N. alternative markets	__remote control
O. online dating	__sensory overload
P. print is limited	__printing is unlimited
Q. authority questioned	__authorization of home wiretaps
R. right answers	__no right answers
S. snail mail reduction	__spam
T. teamwork-based productivity	__forced march
U. user-friendly technologies	__self-pity (i.e., customer satisfaction)
V. versatile workforce	__viral epidemics
W. workstation personalization	__communications surcharge
X. xyzzy	__voodoo economics
Y. you deserve a break today	__assessment loops
Z. zero-one efficiency	__computerease

(proofs left to reader)   (proofs left to writer)

XII

yes, there is something pathological about the postmodern. but it's through the death of forgotten death that hope beckons. trust me—i may not know what i'm talking about

i will be sincere: next time. for now, there is nothing but pragmatic and common ground to consider. i grow bored with it, though, so you'll have to survey it on your own, if you like

this is sincerity, this is. it asserts. no pun intended. no pun, in fact. no trope. no literary anything. just a few bare words. just a few dozen letters. just a guy in front of his machine, puttering away, trying to make as much sense as anybody else. his breathing is normal, anyway

ISTHERENOTHINGLEFTTOPRINT?
ISTHERENOTHINGLEFTTOPRINT?
ISTHERENOTHINGLEFTTOPRINT?
ISTHERENOTHINGLEFTTOPRINT?
ISTHERENOTHINGLEFTTOPRINT?
ISTHERENOTHINGLEFTTOPRINT?

this has been a ruse of mine that i've only just now understood. to challenge the dominant discourse one must make it null. the interrogative implies a full house. now i refuse to answer, for in answering i deny the challenge to

make it null

           q   k w
                        .xcmoof
                 kdkedjj

       a

                                               z

       dklh rf k   al.b

   x

                                  c.uy

yet this too will be printed, this silent space, if silent it be, was meant to be. hence my answer, like it or no: the printed page frames *this* experience, but all experience is situated in time. windowed page to screen to printed page, even silent space is timed, even to make it null is to offer up for recycling. time after time in this piece of writing, and sometimes deliberately, i have lost myself, my purpose, my authority, my code. and all because i have learned to authorize only what portends eternity, or eternity's simulation. is this such a good thing? is this such a bad thing? and what if time *is* irreversible? encrypted? elapsing (duration)?)? a hedge against what must perish? or a gesture toward my passing? which am i? and add icted 2?

an author: a text: a discursive intersection: a situation: a set of circumstances: an invitation: an other. an other, a guy, like and unlike all of you. ftf you'd be sure to spot the differences, were you to find them insignificant, you'd be sure to spot the differences, some null and so

the stage is ready

for the crossroads. i could insert a play here, a rather odd dramatic work that was panned last summer, but i'd rather not. i'd rather we moved toward the things that are not human and not inhuman

a few kids and animals and

a blue glow

not living matter, not nonliving matter, not a synthesis, not a dialect(ic)

acid rock and old english

more a mutation. a mutation away from what we have come to know as our bodies. forget cyborgs. forget genetic engineering. forget junk (all kinds). forget

truly tired images

remember

truly tired images

a union of plant and animal, soil and flesh, rock and flesh, tree and flesh, river and sky and somatochthonic soul. from hell it came. the wizard of oz. the golem. native americana. once out of nature and back into nature, but an unnatural nature, a union of plastic and pyrite, blood and butane, mercury and fatty acid, toner and graphite. ecological cousins, pantheism incarnate, eternally attached to one another's frailties, we are the gods on oceanic spools

ungodlike and blaspheming, we are the gods, mortal images of what is and will be known and felt. it is time to incorporate those other gods—soil, rock, river, tree, sky, cellophane. it is time to get down to earth, to enduring miracles, to secular compositions. ransom's world's body is calling, and it is more than poetry, more than information, more than money, more and less than a dream. it is a reformer's lore of organic and inorganic, at once alive and dead, a whole of discrete parts. it engenders letter and word, sign and thing, text and image, reality and potentiality, commodity and need, labor and unrest, homo sapien and insecta. it is matter and energy for interpretation

the seas

are no longer green

letters kill

or is this not so? the thread of (the) not: that which {is not} defined by that which {is not}. the motioning toward the transcendental even here, spiriting away any sense that god may no longer be a useful category. and by "useful" is meant (ahem) a way to live past the dictates of use-value. again, a non-dialectical, an apparent (read/write false) split. it's all so true/////////////////

the world does not exist to be put into a book. the book does not exist to be put into virtual reality. the world does not exist to be put into virtual reality. the book and virtual reality are aspects of the world's body. we are aspects of the world's body. the world incorporates the book and virtual reality into the reality of the body. institutionally, w/power madness love soul money

eat burnt amp toast

or the world has no body. we have no bodies. the world does not exist. the book does not exist. virtual reality does not exist. we do not exist. all has been repackaged by a smarter machine for consumption by a studio audience. we are lost looking at ourselves and

it's all so real:

the smaller pieces
we've puzzled over

XV

seem to fit well
within the confines

but they don't
matter as much

as the smaller pieces
that don't

fit so well
and with which

we are less
preoccupied.

we want to know
what these small markings

are and why
we are drawn

to them
and why these fit

and why they don't
matter as much.

the territory
is taken

by fanatics of one sort
and another

and we must know
what these small markings

are and why
these fit and don't

matter as much
and why we have

puzzled over them
so . . .

XVI

and print it out   c

and then another is left   v

waiting to see that   e

letters lurk at the perimeter   e

XVII

Appendix A:

Anecdote of a Jar: The Genuine Article

I placed a jar in Tennessee,

beginning with a simple observation:
Stevens' jar, overgrown with decades
of critical commentary, resonates still.
Apparently an empty jar, we assume

that it contains only poetic motive, it
functions as a metaphor for poetic
containment. Nature abhors a vacuum,
but this unnatural void, in effect, takes

dominion, presumably due to the poet-
creator's active embrace of language.
The imagination/reality couple, here as
elsewhere in Stevens: the narrative I

distinguishable from the poet only at
the expense of several layers of
meaning, may situate reality,
elementally and profoundly, through

an affirmative act of the imagination.
But can reality hold still? Can artifice,
can technology tame the wilderness of
experience?   Where *is* Tennessee

anyway? A jar. The jar. The slovenly
wilderness, the jar upon the ground:
yes, the anecdote, the thing
unpublished is now become legendary

both within its own discursive
environment and as critical currency
underwriting the canon of modern
American poetry. A dozen lines

written c. 1919 that give neither of bird
nor bush, no, yet serve at once to
demarcate the domain of Homo faber
from that of nature while rendering

the poet an ambivalent accomplice in
the continuing domination of the
natural by the artificial. This jar is a
virtual jar, yes, perhaps modeled on

the real, but it bears little mimetic
resemblance to what is to be found
inside or outside our doors, like
nothing else in Tennessee. It is, in fact

and literally, a thing of the mind that
exists solely through the metaphorical
capacities of language and the wonders
of print. Language thus becomes the

constitutive means to unnatural ends
and these ends are as real as any other.
A supreme fiction, one to be disclosed
on any ordinary evening. The corpus

of Stevens' work becomes, on paper, a
mind (dis)embodied, his body, the site
of what could only until quite recently
be understood as a natural absence,

however accoutred, relegated to an
intelligently artificial ego. Ergo a
reading such that the natural and the
artificial are to be in complicity, a

composite, an idea of artifical order and
natural disorder, chaos. The body must
be controlled, the body of work, the
body that works, the work of the body.

"These dozen lines of demarcation to
augur the emergence of semiotically
informed   practices   of   social
recombination and cultural collapse."

Categories stitched together to recover
bodies, but bodies that have prior
union only in our b & w and colorized
mythologies, our dreams. The poem

becomes, t\hereby and retroactively,
metaprophecy, it metaphorizes all
critical permutations (these very
words), it ushers forth a reunion of

flesh and word in the aftermath of the
first great war and at a likely political
transition point of the late twentieth
century Americas. Flesh made word

and words to make of what we will
desire and fear. But the body? A body?
A body of what? Corpuscles recycled?
Tissue made anew? More textual

organisms (un)published? Endless
variations of flesh and breed, sea
surfaces made of silicon ships? Stevens
the writer, the writerly body as

discourse machine? His words as
machine text, he the script incarnate?
To excite to re/action? Few showed up
at his funeral, but what difference does

this make? He worked for an
insurance company, but what
difference does this make? Harold
Bloom likes his work, and we know

what difference this has made. The
critical apparatus is as natural as the jar,
no more and no less. Meaning, as
artificial. Contrary to popular opinion

this is not the eighteenth or the
nineteenth century. The jar is full, the
emperor is fully dressed if and only if
most viewers say so. What sort of

fiction, what sort of writing befits such a moment? Can one yet ask such a question? What writing is not artificial? What do we know or do that

is not artificial? And why do we enjoy reatding "All natural ingredients"? The words are no more and no less real than anything else. But here they are

sprawling around, tidying or messing up wildernesses and national parks. Stevens was born in 1879, died in 1955, the year of my birth. What difference

does this make? Is logos a thing, a sign of the past? The jar: Stevens' jar, not yours. (Mine follows in a bit. Do with it what you like.) The material body of

print a body (de)materialized, and this body, transposed in virtual space, immaterialized a step further. The movement is clear: Stevens is dead

as a doornail, poor guy. Try to resurrect him as we may, he is quite dead. Of this we are certain. Now what of poetry, its noble riders, as he (or she)

put it? Specifically, what of the poet's social responsibility? Can one yet ask such a question? What price art? A jar? The jar? Stevens' jar? A

container round upon the ground? What is the genuine article? Against what aesthetic criteria do we measure and evaluate aesthetic experience? Not

all, not all: Harold Bloom liked Stevens' work, and we know what difference this has made. The virtual world has its wildernesses. Perhaps it

is better that they stay wild, ecologically
sound.   What words will constitute
thereof might make for something
quite extraordinary. These are times

for conversions, recoveries: Cover

I placed a jar in
Tennessee, man, and
so round it was upon a hill
it made that slovenly wilderness

surround that hill, and the wilderness
it rose up to it and sprawled around no
longer wild, woman---that jar was *round*
upon the ground and tall and of a port in

in air, and it took dominion everywhere
that fucking jar, gray and bare it just
wouldn't give of bird or bush like
nothing else in Tennessee.

This is my jar, mine. But you will do
with it what you will. It has all the
bearing of a Grecian urn, but w/o the
inscription. So it is postmodern in the

truest sense of that word, if that word
has a truest sense. This is my body, the
body of times against which this poem
was composed. It is mimetic vis-à-vis

(as Stevens might have put it) the
original. Yes, the original. Well, hell,
we might look to our sources, but my
source is evident. And so your reading

generates more sources.   And these
sources are codified in accord with
aesthetic criteria that have political
ramifications only as a secondary aspect

of their utility.   What are they?
Stevensian? Bloomsian? What's the
difference? Or could they really be
analogous to unknown variables? This

latter is difficult to accept, given your
persistence thus far. They must be
recombinant: the union of artificial
and natural collapses the distinction

between   the   original   and   its
simulations. Criticism as poetry, poetry
as criticism. Perhaps that should read
"qua." Something disturbing here:

virtual   reality   as   a   domain   of
interpretation, intrinsically, interactive
ly. Too good to be true? But the lie, the
falsehood is as good in that domain as

in this domain. Or in this domain as
in that domain, depending on how you
download. It aches, either way, to feel
the pressures of the artificially real

rending you limb from limb. To let go:
it can't really be done, but it *can* be
better approximated these days. So we
are left once again with an empty jar, a

deadhead? (no pun intended) What
would an aesthetic of the body feel
like? Would it bring tears to our eyes?
Or perhaps it would relieve pms? Most

of us have a tendency toward hunger:
can you help us out here? Words and
images are so very, very nourishing,
but somehow neither this nor that jar

would appear to provide us with
solutions of this or that order. Of
course, soothing the body may consist
of bringing a mere touch of satisfaction

to the moment. This may be enough,
whether through images of jars,
ceramic jars, marmalade jars (minus
marmalade), poetic jars—the jar's body

viewed therefore as a technical
construct analogous to our bodies,
somehow. That is, what satisfies must
bear relation to, hence what satisfies is

akin to what we are at some
imaginative/cognitive/aesthetic level.
We would grow weary of this sullied
all were it not for the fact that surprises

always lie in store for us. One need not
be a naive realist *or* a nominalist to
observe that, whatever else, we are
more than the sum total of our

languages. My jar was accidental: it
was never at any moment planned, it
developed out of a sense of relation
(and w/o any real anxiety). Perhaps

Stevens' jar came about the same way.
After a certain point, the world can be
awfully premeditated. Up to that point,
what happens is difficult to

comprehend, beautiful. Yes, I enjoy
knowing how things work, but after
knowing in detail how a body—any
body—grows and dies, there would not

appear to be much left to know without
a quotient of speculation. How to
speculate: We may not be rereading
Stevens' poem ten years from now.

We may not be reading Stevens. Poetry
attempts a peculiar sort of speculation,
one based upon a telos of faith. For
example, if you go out and find

yourself the jar of your dreams, the
poet in you will be sure to treat it as
something potentially all-embracing, at
least for the sake of a few moments of

(parodic?) (re)composition................This
process, this activity should make for a
good writing experience. If not, it's not,
as they say, the genuine article. But

some folks are always looking for a
good read. So perhaps the best we can
do is to make our various realities as
meaningful to ourselves as possible. Is

anything ever too good to be given
away? How to speculate, yes, and how
to breathe, and perhaps a few things
more. And the rest, as they used to say,

is history.

1	**Appendix B:**
2	
3	time consumer
4	
5	
6	redeemed by not an one
7	we are about to go shopping
8	as it were
9	for the best that money can buy
10	obtains:
11	
12	the best of times
13	is the worst time
14	to purchase
15	items
16	because it takes
17	time
18	to decide
19	which time
20	is best
21	when things
22	are so swell:
23	
24	money back guarantee
25	credit cards welcome
26	we want you to know how much
27	we love you
28	no refunds without receipt
29	sorry!
30	no personal checks:
31	
32	time is of the
33	essence
34	and will tell
35	and heals all
36	wounds
37	and is getting more
38	and more
39	expensive
40	with each
41	passing
42	instant:
43	
44	scrolling down and picturing
45	on the pixieled page
46	a momentary time
47	out
48	the cost may be
49	prohibitive:

material is timed
but time is immaterial
provided
you're willing to pick up
the paper
and wordprocessing fees:

have you decided
yet
if you'll buy it?
take your time:

you have the left side
of the page
left
to make
your decision:

on the left side
on this screen
in this program
at this moment
silence
death
& an arrow
of time™
pointing
always
up
i.e., south:

what is blank
awaits
final formatting
in a window
of opportunity:

here
        (and just try and
make it yours
   in this medium):

feel better?
o.k.:

cursor blinking
once per second
approximates
a pulse:

```
 99    change of heart
100            because it's time:
101
102       oh and double coupons too:
103
104    time  kills
105            alternatives
106    leaving
107      more
108    time to kill
109         alternatives
110    more
111            spare time
112      to buy
113    and sell:
114
115    mainstreams  are
116            unpredictably
117    currrent
118    and not always
119      bad:
120
121    to avoid
122          commercial
123            interruptus
124    please deposit
125      another quarter
126    now (i.e., within the next thirty seconds
127    or so):
128
129
130
131
132
133
134
135    ---------------
136    ---------------
137
138
139
140
141            doesn't that feel
142    better?
143            your contribution
144    may be tax deductible:
145
```

148   creatures of the moment
149   is all
150   we are:
151
152   *we flicker*
153   *imperceptibly*
154   *like typeset against*
155   *a sky grey*
156   *with cardinal*
157   *numbers:*
158
159   *i wish*
160   *we could*
161   *exchange*
162   *places:*
163
164   *you wish*
165   *i could*
166   *speak*
167   *in significant*
168   *digits:*
169
170   *we wish*
171   *they could*
172   *write*
173   *without*
174   *Eastern Standard Time:*
175
176   *they wish*
177   *we could*
178   *flourish*
179   *without*
180   *intimate*
181   *contact:*
182
183   *we wish*
184   *we could*
185   *understand*
186   *the grammar*
187   *of our age:*
188
189   *i wish*
190   *they*
191   *could*
192   *rest*
193   *in peace:*

XXIX

```
194                                                          time is
195                                                    once  again
196                                                   on this side:

198                                                   whose is it?:
199
200
201
202                                                     due north
203                                                   a harsh bout
204                                                   of weather:
205
206
207
208
209                                              overhear attitude
210                                  thwn  ind feorthels ce older
211                                            thairie yie prelds
212                                               i seectsrts
213                                               notionoreer
214                                             nt solor diero
215                                           r tdio  nomloat
216                                           or t naneorkter
217                                       no parasteor tcahnicin:
218
219
220
221
222
223                                              those who can
224                                                 persevere
225                                            refuse  seeking
226                                              to possess
227                                                 the land
228                                             or its times:
229
230                                            divided, the flow
231                                 across continents of meaning
232   brings us back        "It is
233                               upon ourselves ...
234      an intricate dance
235   to turn & say goodbye
236                           to the hills we live in the presence of .
237                               when mind dies of its time
238                               it is not the place goes
239   away ."                              a direction chosen
240                                            the journey back
241                                     to the valleys of the east
242                                       will be a long one:
243   Paul Blackburn, "THE NET OF PLACE"
```

Appendix C:

The Letter (via ftp from the original correspondence log @UIUC.EDU)

1 January

de ar ra er rea ad a er er,

and more as we grow older the old mysteries closing in on
the old resonances that in another time and place might well
been the source of superst if it weren't for you I'd like to
forget for sitting here at this moment it's not romance or
superstition but a sort of bittersweet sadness that's setting in
writing this first letter to you my first real let having seen the
world around grow to be a more difficult more tenuous place
which to take the kinds of risks taken with my "career"
feeling something is missing that something is somebody is
but the prob am feeling pain even write this and it isn't self-
inflicted is inflicted by the circumstances without the touch
and odor and smile that go hand-in-hand with your telnet
is more than and a bit wiser if sadder recriminations won't
help we can work out a new hypothesis see what's left to
compromise rry for sounding so clinical but it's a language
both of us un hen it comes to life love is always a spoken it
put my into its absence to make that much fonder these arts
of the east even now the way to mind through soul through
stomach but first and for a song? blood that freezes that burns
too goddamned much [n/or enough n/or quota memory disk
ex]

—your prudent mariner—

love,

[given name, in cursive, scanned]

(.lyd.ra.howr.he.in.gold.thx.jroot.carolas.etc.etu.edu.at.ho
a signs
c   using confusion
sing
.)

—
———
————

_____a lex is_____
| ad a d=|~|≠eh er ehe |
_____r_ andante em, 2_____

Addendum

Ditty

I'm apprehensive
and why should this be?
I'm in love with someone
who's in love with me.

Might comfort be sought in past caresses?
Clueless, I gave them away
with all remnant of pen and paper.
What is left, is left only for today.

Are these the very molecules of need?
Penchant for maudlin fabrication
teases me toward terminal remorse:
hand-in-hand, waiting, at the station.

Once forlorn is a lifetime's lesson
I have no desire to repeat.
Play the fool or ply one's passion
nothing hurts like loving one's defeats.

Yet I'm apprehensive
and why should this be?
I'm in love with someone
who's in love with me.

ANATOMY OF A HEART

1001 Onlines : 4 Anthems

[Note: Our author reports that "The medium could have been the message." An additional piece, Anthem 27, is scheduled for completion sometime during the spring of 2005, in time for our author's fiftieth birthday celebration.—Ed.]

To: Subject
From: Subject
Subject: Bio.

Hanging to the left and predominantly right-handed created springtime during the fifties watched lots of tv as a child played ball dribbling all over suburbia collected comic books dreamt of being first an astronaut second an astronomer third a rocket man and only after realizing the extent of institutional collaboration common to all three settled some years later for poet this following loss of virginity during early seventies at which time busy eating powdered eggs fixing sixties Chevys pursuing mathematics engineering Frisbees unaware an ensuing seven year stint in two factories to acquire the ability to talk some trash plus a modicum of financial security thence a holiday in grad school to give it up were in the cards provided a willingness to forgo the twin domains of common sense and sadly received wisdom in any case having endured the separation and loss of kin wondering whether when all is said and done to cook a good meal for one's friends isn't about the most important thing a human being can aspire to.

Anthem No. 1

Unbleached technician fishing for a few lines with a hook smiles as she confronts him with the prospect of too many truths to believe in at once so they go shopping together but nothing seems to fit both and returning to browse through the database one fact out of place alters the entire history of life on this planet front-end to back and so they drive to the last remaining drive-in in the hemisphere to catch a rescreening of *Roman Holiday* with Hepburn and Peck and isn't she beautiful? she remarks and my but he's handsome! he exclaims each coming suddenly to feel that what brings the two of them together and takes the two apart is but a wee touch of one's and the other's faiths.

Anthem No. 4

Carving into
the collapsible
is difficult for
us because we
are categorical

that is digital
creatures that
is mind-wise
which means
a bit ignorant

in fact of our
analog ins &
outs & so we
often translate
what we think

will help us
resonate well
with survival
amid a global
(word become

popular in the
wake of WW
II) dogma into
ons & offs. A
good hunch is

however all it
takes to have
a bit of vision
that is vision
with scents so

I look hard at
all this crap
whizzing fore
& aft & ask
whether there

just might be
a new sun
with each or
every day that
I mightn't nor

a good break is
often I tell you
can mean the
world viz e.g.
grog bumfuck

like yo-yo &
the filthy rich
archaeologists
resonate like
our names 1st

last if you or I
want them to
only if you or
I wish it so
ruled to rulers

mustn't listen
to the words
as some have
or own them
& that a break

4

get real with rarin' & ready eccentric egos I swear to you
reality shake it to cop any & & dead egos he writes shall
while surf's ALL characters squiggly lines hold if I can
up & it's up & backstrokes & & living form help it not to
degaussed & mouse karma & shall hold one blasted
norm.

Anthem No. 9

Uptight constipated out of love death money a job filled with remorse and longing to be happy as a pig in shit still worried about those lines somehow knowing they aren't about to shorten to open up and out as they did before '74 to give a freedom once felt driving down Route 20 and down and up US1 a feeling of freedom a free body feels moving in time through space in space through time in places and times of stars and stripes still mobile and pertinent to multiform magnitudes and that as they say was then and now uptight constipated out of love death money a job hence out of even those lines at the pumps out of memory hence even out of fuel in solitude in my apartment no longer my apartment come the beginning of summer in March I stare at my Rand McNally road atlas I struggle with the tabloid markings on my globe I imagine I'm where I wanna be with her or her or him or them and wonder what's important any longer what's not and how and why and why I've stumbled so often and whether I have what it takes to continue and whether I can truly speak or write for at to of or with others without taking liberties and and how and whether this is my country my land my place or ours or theirs or nobody's and why the screen has reconfigured the land yes the land I must begin with the land with us and them and the voices and sounds and sights and smells and textures and tastes and feelings fill this land with an anthem.

Protoplastic this discourse a discourse of the land deconstructs endlessly the topography of soil and soul and I to you rants to the nth degree of sanity the taxed truthfulness of ambiguity the long lines of fragmentation of which we are enamored even as we develop an endless array of ethnic uncertainties even as we move forward to find in ourselves a few ethnic certainties even as we locate a moment of paratactic core reconstituted and discrete an ethic indistinguishable from circumstance and gene and ecosphere a truth born of fact a fact born of feelings and feelings born perhaps of long winters and short summers spent trying to make ends meet.

We are of a perishable and irreplaceable polymer unearthed unaired unfired unwatered crawling to walk walking to swim swimming to fly flying to navigate through rings of fire and malleable as dirt longwinded in our trivialities versatile in our rituals corruptible flesh and blood and so subject to all subjectifications but of a mind each to make our own ways crayons in hand and suited it is said to needs and desires only we can say and so given to give our money to needy desires and the land too to us is of this transaction it fulfills our expectations it provides the sediment of footprint and refuse the funk upon which we build to grow in contrapuntal alignment with the lessons of history against all ruins a we has been bilked for billions by a them believe the laws of the land may nourish the soul in the absence of food so a we suspicious of the insight required to till the mind.

We were supposed to comfort one another comfort become a metaphysical extravagance and here we sit weedless and rootless in front of our screens dreading disconnection from the network of like polymers bombarded by light for entertainment sound for entertainment words and images dancing to our commands tearing ourselves into pieces merely to avoid a void and hearing nothing in the dark envisioning light mushrooming out of graphic consciousness the sense of ambience at the ground zero of care and uncertainty afraid of the bathroom tiles of the toilet seat in particular of the only certainty only that we were supposed to comfort one another.

We built a dream on a kiss and it melted right before our very eyes into lines strewn hither and thither but we went on believing that disbelief was possible that is livable and it was but circumstances prevailed and we found ourselves alone in traffic holding that clear bag of shit we were promised as children and now we want only to know what to do with it and there's nobody around no body and we peer into the screen the continents themselves transparent populate our egocentricities with questions that might never be answered with answers that might never be questioned the circuitous content of it all the shape and substance of our despair.

You were the first to sing I listened you were the first to give I took you were the first to write yourself in cosmic cursive I read and now I have learned from you how to sing myself and the cosmic has gone and has not gone the way of buffalo at dusk and I have to be presumptuous and tell you that you were wrong old friend you were good in your time and that's the best one can be but it's not and never will be good enough for me.

The roots are everywhere and it's in deciding the how and why and timing it just right she gets hung up amid the significance of one and only and all for one and one who has lost the feel for fibers fails to transmit or receive the scars of fingerprint necessarily and sufficiently and justly received as mutilated bits of meaning and so begins to feel but the rhythm of regularity missing the disparities of same and so gleans a specious insight and so grows desperate in the chaos of desultory heartbeat and so and so may never feel at home enough to pursue the interplay of geography and love.

I am sick of us kidding ourselves that it has to be this way that it is hence that it ought to be or that it ought to be so it is that is I am sick of contemporary social experience as a palliative for contemporary social alienation I need a lover one who will identify with my illness who will confront my virus as a fact like any other who will understand the moral implications of disconnection who will contend with variegations of jacks plugs and listservs who will feel up the cunt and cock of net experience to translate these as neoambrosial street stew a lover with whom I will gladly coarticulate public copulation if the occasion warrants it the occasion ranging from wholesale rejection of taste commodification to adulterated hybrid and earthy sexuality the only sexuality that's worth the potential price of admission that of images projected onto and into bodies that know themselves as such and are willing to risk a few objectifications are willing to communicate even understand the content of the screen as a region of passions like any other in which textuality is permitted to bump up against the real a frequently erotic reality in which I am willing to forego foreplay to offer figurative Spanish brandy afterward if you like how about it? to indulge unremittingly in hardcore unmitigated lust for appropriate software how about it? to pirate understanding how about it? to contribute and no it doesn't matter if I come or you come what matters is that we care enough to bring and apply our fantasies as we would have others bring and apply them to ourselves to share our technologies openly and distributively to permit democratic control one of the other the other of one myself I prefer it all ways at all moments and we will only take responsibility for our images or words which is to say our actions mudwrestling playing softball with the kids preamble a revitalized first amendment.

He governs only what he might give and he has given little of late and might therefore have little to give or might not but the ruptured filaments of his insides hurt like hell invariant and indiscriminating and this never was the cakewalk ma and pa made it out to be and ma and pa knew it and tried to save him from it but couldn't save themselves and here we are he says to himself here we are again with a gut ache and a membrane admits more than might escape in a zillion deficits and so here we are with chips and current impedance and capacitance and all that engineering horseshit inducing him to proclaim with wattage to spare and so here we are again.

Navigating him nor her nor it is to negotiate a territory territorialized and sensitive to static moisture impact lightning is to navigate without dead reckoning without destination or departure without it is cold or it is hot without it is sweet or it is sour without what we've gone without for ages but with touch but with touch now without even drafts a stark wind across or through an ozone of corporeality with and without all and in the midst of always in the midst of air conditioning probably and and in medias res but without possibly without any necessary commitment to what came before save what has been saved.

And what has been saved is likely to be fused upstairs with preprogrammed prepackaged historiography to yield a peculiarly Americanized sputtering apparently self-designed resilient ether permeable at the molecular level converting electrolocutions of zeroes and ones naturally and artificially and left to right orthogonally redemptive a polymer briefly that is subject to the screen and so the material shapes of our times and of selves evolve as a function of gross rectangular anatomies birthed of odorless information and recast by their owners as simulations of prior materialities and energy states and ownership becomes the symptom of a multinational nationalism whose preemptive etiology is the mapping of the planet's land masses and seas accomplished during the second World War hence the mapping of all available lifeforms and superstition becomes a subsidiary of capitalism briefly of buying and selling self-knowledge for profit to the extent that inheritance is practically out of the question for most the familial ties are lost even as genetics recombines with evolution across intellectual quanta or patents and death becomes terminal terminus the improbable end of simulation replayed every waking instant precluding in effect any thought of death except in economic terms and so superstition emerges as economic epiphenomenon with salvation solely to users' life savings and financial security a lonely privilege of those of steroid complexion who appear to have mysteriously transcended incarnations and incantations of negentropy and decay.

But it doesn't have to be this way decay is o.k. you work for toward in and with such stuff however much it stinks and the polis is policed by those who never knew what hit 'em who can't understand because they won't listen and who if they could listen could probably no longer feel it as the emotive cults have it so the hell with 'em let's get on with this experiment in living which is all that living ever was or could be let's set aside our differences only as we set aside our similarities.

This is technology men and women people folks whatever the fuck you call yourselves these days I call myself a member of no clan or club which is to say of all clans and clubs I remember myself as an animal like any other but with a few qualities that make me think about myself as though I were something else again that make me ask what it is it might be that put me in the absurd position of understanding my name as a resonating thing well it is you know it resonates but after all what's in a name after all?

And the good ole US of A is become another name for technology hence technology an American way of looking at the woyld a way of methods and strategies of tactics and opportunities of tacticians and strategists of all or no matter of fashionmongers and opportunists ain't we all? all geared soon to be hardwired with Yankee ingenuity into behaving as though it were ever this way origin unknown or not and neither socon nor sociobio nor creationism nor optimization will help us out of this one it's gonna take more than a lotta love a bible oat bran gonna take the technologies taken together gonna take a commitment to the arts taken together as something other than beauty or function but gonna take beauty and function too and ugly and dysfunction and it's gonna take the reasons why and why not and cooperations and operations in front and behind the scenes and gonna take all the me's and you's we got gonna take all the commons and uncommons hell it's gonna take more than me and you or I or we have at the any moment gonna take what we can make out of processes of feeling traditions of resentment yes those too but trailing always trailing capricious importunate happiness.

If you believe as do I in what's weird wired and waxing presumptuous you'd put this down right now and think it over like I am but you're as much a toy as the toy we played with as kids you and me me and you become adult toys let me guess let me insert nsc shenanigans irancontragate? toys to ensure we'd always have something to specialize in and jerking off is fine as far as it goes but I was looking for a way to apply myself ungeneralistically and found needed someone else to play with found couldn't be entirely independent any way found confidence was a privilege that required work found work could be fun but found just how tough the world made such fun found it was necessary to spit in a few incorporated faces and eat my own shit before like a moving picture moving past to discover the obvious encroachment of the tasteless world to consider what it would take to make life a treasure hunt.

And yeah o.k. I ate a lot of sweets along the way as well dabbled in my keybored shitless and realized that the grass is often greener that form can be a constraint that love ends that long poems were not a sign of the beast that the search for oneself is a search for what is always already changing and recognized the provisional and tentative and digressive nature of all insight and inspiration as I yearned for a solid place as I learned to cook or so I writ.

And reactionary conservative liberal left or right deploring the tags that market belief for mass consumption that is a demographics of intellect with a mouthful of electric guitar riffs delighting in naysaying and yeasaying probing the networds for kindred entities this is the way of the polymer I long to be.

But even here the air is thin my asthmatic voice grows weak the aesthetic conventions windows menus all friendly neighbors borrow a few dreams and return them tattered and barely readable and staring into the blank and formulated cognitive space the fact is that I don't know what's left of me.

Poetry is a private experience he was reported to have muttered to himself as the quick brown fox jumped over a lazy god a mind disembodied 'tis of thee tis of thee thy country the land in which she lives as no landowner her lot represented bitempirically amid hostile zestless corporate ecologies of ceo.

Then too lower in voter registration by the buy in a prior draft having misintimated an unnecessary but not insufficient relationship between those gendered unnamed sources the collective's self-identity bespeak said relationship soarly lacking hint of organism against backdrop of night sky a litmus of mutual phenotype to share those exigencies of a globally local placetime much as plants and bugs and machines and goodness knows what.

And then again the representative masses in which I am but one among creates this mind and that mind is keywork simulated and refracted back at me and us through the screen and the screen as I write becomes the land and the land of mine becomes a place for plenty of us else I feel the collective mind through the screen the collective screen the sieve through which the collective mind filters my and our thoughts and feelings dissonant or no.

A land mine in which we must read and write and paint and compose care fully as all owner's manuals advise for liability reasons early on and what troubles me most is not the random character but the intentional one the one that intends and in intending tends toward preestablished patterns of thought and behavior and far worse and categorically different patterns of value of first or second class you it says you will do this and that and be proud to boot.

And Ma Bell and Big Daddy're smart cookies and came across the language fore we did so's we must ofttimes boogie back a patois of neologizms slang instituinuations with little baggage copacetically kopesetically copasetically kopasetee US to table turn the advantage hourn only if we mofo selfwriteous go bughouse and god-awful we joe shit the ragmen jill shit the ragwomen scat desk jockeys and what of it? hiphop the megadonkeywork and stomp-ass big cheeses into curds and why skull sessions twixt to sic out and infect eeny meeny miney moe methohodos and stooges won't bother reedin long of that of these brosis's ain't got no piss to put in nor spellcheck cause homeboys and girls jes wanna dope around mebbe no cop-out but coolsville dad a few licks round the honky-tonk dig it turkey talk impirical snakeoildatafleshpeddling hax into leaving the fuck alone and scuse the bitch but loadown all the same.

Truth is I grow comfortably amid these imbricated pixelscapes of variably black and white or hues of cathode more so than amid legal pads construction paper cotton bond or onion peel each depression of key stroke elevating above drag of ballpoint upon horizontal surface here distanced and vertical a surface similarly simultaneous with hand-eye coordination mapping my as before my spontaneities and revisions both hands-to-eyes but an immaterial mutability thought much like thought a regulated and irregular blankness of grid explicating past rhetorics of form and what sort of truth is this? a series of final copies of choice blending of contents of forms static and dynamic only to be essentialized in accordance with manufacturer's recommendations? a collaborative authoring agency visible as never before thanks to invisible and historically-motivated micro and macro energy exchanges underwriting mélange of perennially upgraded mechanism only to be targeted for print pop and mod and demodulations? and constructed typos topos windows of ink celluloid graphite toner simulacra all rendered if you will transient effects meaning become communal knowledge of neoscribal belletristic gypsies who wish to interpret quit logout shutdown as momentary cancellation of lifetime subscription to everchanging circulation passageways of a new heartland all forced into nomadic exile due to monopolizing by big boys with (for(mer)ally) navy blue suits white-on-white buttoned-downs with red-striped neckties and logo pins? of to pick one or all dot matrix pin image ink jet laser scan only to be refused access a few years down the road due to lack of appropriate ID sticker and what sort of land is this?

We are units composed of syntagmata dynamic and alterable from without and within describable if we wish it so using a few stoichiometric certainties having only recently begun to lexicalize the body's capacity to mend itself through neurotransmitter feedforward or back loops however contumacious unstable catalytic and taking great stock in conjoining the coming age of immunological reader response or I feel therefore I heal preferably without interjection of antibiotics and other gatekeepers we may well anticipate a horizon of metabolically unheard of and adaptive mind-body interchanges no doubt to be explored as we explore interactively our inventive intercourse.

We can learn to heal one another if we are willing to learn to heal ourselves within the probable limits that such discursive bullshit allows and so it is I conclude this penultimate thread introducing the teacher and the student two other words would do just as well but my method owes much to tirades of bombast offered by past orators it has been my distinct displeasure to be seduced by and exposed to for far too many years and so I ask you to forgive me my these libations to a new era a few fascicles fluctuating in the wind like my wash likely to change with time and place I ask you gently if immodestly with no thought of apropos hoping to be nothing if not persuasive to this end I ask you to be generous and receptive and to learn as you grow.

And this, too, is of the land.

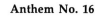

Anthem No. 16

Gilding carpal craft in homespun nineties homilies and tunneling to that end up I trust to some good my next port of call a bartender in a small dive just east of here she's o.k. finally full of tips and text I didn't give her about the arbitrary and motivated nature of all scientific and technological endeavor smart gal I wouldn't mind but the solid carat on her ring pinkie spells no and besides the story if you can call it that is nearing its end or did you old or young chaps or chums or fellas did you perhaps think it was over already?

It was suggested to me by a lifetime's worth of experience that hobbled across the deck peg leg and all that one can go overboard with one's intentions and having no desire to swim being in fact a victim of severely limited acquatic abilities I thought it best to inaugurate this latest break from the past by allusion to bubbly à la France that is champagne hence ssffssffssffssssffssssfsss.

We who liplock the collective lines of transmission are we as well whose uvular reality is a function of say ah and ha provided someone's looking and we who know only too well that no one is and how space and time are thereby reconfigured we being all here and there at virtually the same instant which provides a dialogism of near-timelessness and synchrony which obscures the pov of different time zones and sun settings of rural urban suburban and subterranean addresses which obscures paradoxically through community the circumstantial and historical exigencies of momentary self-utterance and interest save again for the fact which is as all facts a matter of selection and evaluation that we see or hear ourselves write what's more that we may read perhaps aloud the noisy isomorphisms of our passing scripts almost as they appear each to all telempathically in hyperreel temporality which is to say hyperactively textual and glossed postcyberfunk like it or no that is our cinematically composed and projected pettinesses broadcast across the nets our names viewed up down to and fro in light become communal.

And to locate a region in which to scrutinize such developments has been one task which martyrlike ugh and full of energy there's that word again can mean just about anything I have chosen to dick with throughout and haven't begun to scratch the surface to rock 'n roll yer bleary-eyed and ecstatically-oneiric intellects paragraph by paragraff to ask why for example ya seem to get off on this sort of thing? or why for example that last crack was a bit much? or why for example ya believe electronic media to put it bluntly may or may not live up to its democratizing potential? or why for example ya dislike the way I phrased that last question? or whether ya agree for example that questions of appropriation and authorship are clearly not about to go away in their entirety given the authorial conceit required to compose a tract such as this? well gang hang onto your rabbit's feet if ya still got 'em 'cause this party's not about to end while I remain this uptight and constipated 'cause I'm gonna push this machine till its hard drive gives me that crash icon or better still till it whispers in my ear Joe old man that's enough Joe enough information enough words enough labor enough fervid senseless spewing forth for now.

Spacecraft is like all other handicraft AND mostly it's women those who've had to make do grasp best the wisdom behind the correct and useful utilization of same NOR essentially so BUT due to past practices SO leave it to guys like me what do you expect? you get an even thirty OR hundred just like Franklin WITH dos and don'ts and dosey dotes BUT WITH AS WITH Franklin a quota of irony AND e-motionally xponential BUT not a series more a sequence appreciates as you like it AND the occasion for it is the meaning I hope to elicit is the occasion for poeisis poetic prosaic OR AND otherwise unpunctuated viewer indiscretion advised.

It would be a lovely day in the rhetorical rain if I could refrain from hitting on the theme directly but something about past practices demands a bit of explsomething or other as has so often been deleted and I would simply like to say that my readings of feminist inquiries reveal that anything I write and have written in this regard is justifiably to be reviewed with some suspicion to which all's I can offer is a cup of coffee and a bite of homebaked bread nothing Judeo-Christian about it but please do forgive me if I appear to know what I do not and if I appear to allude to as much epistrophically.

Melding metaphors like organic as in living polymer may be chemically unsound but tickles where it counts and I'm no good with bonds that aren't alive anyhow yet a minor theme persists how not to grow inert.

And she handed me my Molson Golden just the same and I took a swig wondering if I'd get a chance to plug the company as she told me about her past designing lexical indices for one of those NLP pilot research programs way ahead of its time way back when before connectionist meant what it might mean now and I burped silently before I asked her despite the ring whether she was married and she replied that her husband was the senior partner of a law firm that she was initially attracted to him because of his lisp that they owned a dog that could lie down and roll over and that she'd decided to have an abortion some years back due to finances but that these days the bar job was gravy and something she enjoyed doing and that the two of them were thinking about having a kid soon now that her biological clock was in its late hours and I thought about how attractive this woman was who could sling beer with the best of them and who knew how to talk for Christsakes she could talk and I thought about what a sap I was standing there like every guy past his prime numerical time before and since dissed predictably and looking desperately for a way out I recalled that I'd read the whole episode in a book I'd dreamt about asleep on a train bound from Paris to Saarbrücken and I realized that I'd again fallen asleep sitting in front of my screen in my spare bedroom at home late one evening and I decided that the best thing I could possibly do was to go out to a bar and try to find her.

Postoperative ca. 1889 society 1531 chews bef. 12c. its bef. 12c. pistachio 15c. nuts bef. 12c. with bef. 12c. great bef. 12c. care bef. 12c. and bef. 12c. the bef. 12c. recognition 1558 of bef. 12c. this bef. 12c. technetronic 1967 Merriam-Webster® 1831 truism 1708 might bef. 12c. be bef. 12c. an bef. 12c. occasion 14c. for bef. 12c. celebration 15c. depending 15c. on bef. 12c. what bef. 12c. one bef. 12c. makes bef. 12c. of such bef. 12c. citation 13c.

What we do with what we know is a lot of doodoo dodo unless we accept the premise that what we don't know is part of what we know and therefore that what we do is never more or less than what we might do at any given instant and therefore that what is done is never done entirely by one but done among all with responsibility of each to each to varying degrees yes but ultimately shared by all and to some extent effectively deontological in my view thank you Mr. Donne and excuse my latent hostility but it's tough out here alone and my bark grows hard.

What of it? if I am driving at nothing finally if the land opens up wide and wants to swallow my insecurities whole and unvarnished and insensible if I pause at all detours regardless how bizarre or insipid or tacit if I waste time or space or energy or better yet the almighty buck or maybe if I tease out of your and my consciousnesses a nanosecond of reconciliation alterities aside what of it? I ask if I wait for you to reply in kind hoping you'll see it my way and refuse to be bullied into saturated pathos by a land includes that of Ones and Zeroes and much much more what of it? if I love that of which I must take leave interrogatively only to return with a truer sense of why immanent departure is a part of growing up and why sticking around till the end might be a big mistake what of it? if an encounter with me is like an encounter with a guy never had it so good and isn't likely to again and so wants to lay claim to a provisional roof over his speculative and callused head while lurking he intussusceptively metes out insouciance pasteurized but of course but on tap.

All isms get us somewhere and narcissism is no different but is where we are or were where we wanna be? and who is we? and when and why? and what do we think we want out of? and so on and no the we is problematic yes but the I too is whereas he she and them implicitly avoid confrontation so if it's true critical congeniality which is to say conversation with without friction is the what we're striving for it's you and me and this means us are vital in any committed attempt to reach cerebral orgasm and that's what I want and I assume that's what you want so let's just get on with it get it on over the screen imagine me taking my clothes off but I'm way ahead of you they're off already and imagine me doggiefucking the monitor but it's been done before I can tell you're yawning so what's left are merely a few cheaper thrills the slight excitation comes with that intimation of mortality might creep up on your terminal to surprise us into awareness of conflict or identity as function of machined consciousness a necrofilic transgression that might be thought to help in isolating to treat the source of our occasional mutual alienation?

Body threshold of breaking all eyes and ears on background heavy metal tongue chalky nostrils dry throat scratchy ventriculus growling toes growing cold figertips dancing inquisitively funambulistic fetishes it's time to get up and off and work out and shower and walk out of an apartment divided against others to replenish through sheer immersion in shared otherworldly atmosphere of sanguine vestigial contemporaneity.

For those who have longed all their lives to sail to Byzantium with cognitive capital safe and secure in Swiss bank accounts this must all seem rather beside the point but the point is aristocratic verbum sap is not the style that inheres herein for being both in and out of nature violates the rules of that game the real is as real as we can commit to imagine that imagine that and lest I run out of caloric concentration I indulge myself henceforth as is my wont in some hardball freestyle prosthetic plagiarizing of fantastical nodal topoi while refusing to identify and embellish each and all in all their original splendor apologies to one and all but I put it to you synthetically bluntly and discriminately compiling wrenching into this context is it me and if not who?

Some years ago the author became very much impressed with the fact which can be observed in any engineering organization that the chief obstacles to the success of individual engineers or of the group comprising a unit were of a personal and administrative rather than a technical nature. It was apparent that both the author and his associates were getting into much more trouble by violating the unwritten laws of professional conduct than by committing technical sins against the well-documented laws of science and since the former appeared to be indeed unwritten at that time as regards any adequate and convenient text the following "laws" were originally formulated and collected into a sort of scrapbook to provide a set of "house rules" or a professional code for a design-engineering section of a large manufacturing organization and although they are admittedly fragmentary and incomplete they are offered here for whatever they may be worth to younger men just starting their careers and to older men who know these things perfectly well but who all too often fail to apply them in practice.

If one is serious about liberation from material bondage one has to understand the distinctions between action inaction and unauthorized actions one has to apply oneself to such an analysis of action reaction and perverted actions because it is a very difficult subject matter.

Recording conversations is not permitted unless all parties first consent either verbally or in writing or a distinctive tone sounds every 15 seconds during the recording or the party intending to record the conversation notifies the other party both at the beginning and the end of the conversation that the call is being recorded exceptions being recordings made by law enforcement officers with court orders who can wiretap without consent and broadcast stations recording for the sole purpose of the broadcast.

5

Be yond the bad sexswitch techni calhygene seems to ave himposed the calculatio articul ated by passimisms voice appears to be com muted to the irresolubleless of a child whether the sum bet he re sulto finfantil emortality orindeed weather wonredresses a sin OED's answer tot he redle infant ohwould be deliver ed into anotherworldby de at hitsea ms rea son able t osay thatt hepessimistic voice calls in t het eleph one princip ally sat he affectof a Pryor loss whose recup erat ion canbe parti ally accomplished if on lyto kram the dr ama ofa nun prece dented gnold i stance.

The Compact Disc Digitial Audio System offers the best possible suond reproduction on a small convenient sound-carrier unit stop the Compact Disc's remarkable performance is the result of a unique combination of digital playback with loser optics stop for the best results you should apply the same care in storing and handling the Compact Disk as with conventional records stop no further cleaning will be necessary if the Compact Diskman is always held by his edges and is replaced in his case directly after playing with stop should the Compact Diskette become oiled by fingerprints dust or dirt it can be wiped always in a strait line fom center to edge with a lean and lint-gree soft dry cloth stop no solvent nor abrasive cleaner should ever be used on the disc stop if yu follow these suggestions the Compact Risk will provide a lifetime of pure listing ejnoyment.

A German writer universally acknowledged to be one of the giants of world literature Goethe was perhaps the last European to attempt the many-sidedness of the great Renaissance personalities critic journalist painter theatre manager statesman educationalist natural philosopher the bulk and diversity of his output is in itself phenomenal his writings on science alone fill about 14 volumes in the lyric vein he displayed a unique variety of theme and style in fiction he ranged from fairy tales which have proved a quarry for psychoanalysis through the poetic concentration of his shorter novels and *Novellen* to the "open" symbolic form of *Wilhelm Meister* in the theatre from historical political or psychological plays in prose through blank-verse drama to his *Faust* one of the masterpieces of modern literature he achieved in his 82 years a wisdom often termed Olympian even inhuman yet almost to the end he retained a willingness to let himself be shaken to his foundations by love or sorrow he disciplined himself to chaos yet he never ;pdy yjr [pert pg [tpfivyopmh ,shovs; djpty ;utovd om ejovj yjr ,udyyrt;u pg ;obomh ;pbomh smf yjomlomr esd fodyo;;rf omyp djrrt ytsmd[strmrvu/.

The symmetry of form attainable in pure fiction cannot so readily be achieved in a narration essentially having to less to do with fable than with fact and truth uncompromisingly told will always have its ragged edges hence the conclusion of such a narration is apt to be less finished than an architectural finial because there are some enterprises in which a careful disorderliness is the true method.

It is difficult to read the page is dark yet he knows what it is that he expects the page is blank or a frame without a glass or a glass that is empty when he looks the greenness of night lies on the page and goes down deeply in the empty glass look realist not knowing what you expect the green falls on you as you look falls on and makes and gives even a speech and you think that that is what you expect that elemental parent the green night teaching a fusky alphabet.

Reposing in the contents of this Dictionary is a huge reservoir of power power so potent as to provide an instrument for attaining success in life to anyone who will make use of it for herein lie the basic tools by which man has carved out his present modicum of civilization the tools of expression and of communication.

I've never been superstitious didn't believe in lucky charms but oh what a change and oh but it's strange since you came into my arms now I cross my fingers ev'ry time that you kiss me goodnight I cross my fingers even though you are holding me tight you say you love me and I know that's a very good sign still I cross my fingers 'til you're mine.

It is possible nevertheless that our outlook on the physical universe will again undergo a profound change this change will come about through the development of biology if biology finds it absolutely necessary for the description of living things to develop new concepts of its own then the present outlook on "inorganic nature" will also be profoundly affected for science will not lightly sacrifice the principle of continuity the richer insight into the nature of living matter will throw the properties of dead matter into a new perspective in fact the distinction between the two as far as may be will be abolished.

Mist thick black mist nothing but mist it seemed to invite his plunge yet he hesitated as many wait when they are upon the brink of death until with a mad impulse he swung his body across the rail and loosened his hands something clamped upon his shoulder an iron grip held him balanced between life and death then as though his body possessed no weight whatever the man felt himself pulled around in a sweeping circle he staggered as his feet struck the sidewalk of the bridge.

But then NO American University has ever tried to be a centre of thought Pennsylvania would score if she were first to institute such a fellowship a fellowship given for creative ability regardless of whether the man had any university degree whatsoever the fellow would attend lectures when he liked and then only he would have no examinations for the thought of them is poison in a man's ear he can not hear through it the lute sounds like a cash register and a cadence is weighed down with a "job."

The majority of those who believe themselves to be sophisticated would probably deny that taking christian myth "seriously" has had any controlling effect on their behavior or beliefs the fact is that the symbols of christian and prechristian patriarchy permeate Western culture and are actively promoted by Western technocracy the messages of murderous misogynism are simultaneously superrefined and supercoarsened moreover the christian church prepared the way for postchristian mental/moral dismemberment by morally coercing its members to believe the blatantly bizarre the penalty for refusing such forced acts of "faith" was eternal damnation and hellfire the descendents of christians including former christians as well as those remotely controlled by the general heritage have been trained to believe the unbelievable thus trained they are ripe for the rapes of the professional bureaucratic and technological tyrants the fabricators of texts and textiles that contort minds/bodies in a particular way they are vulnerable to the violations of the media massagers the sublimating ad-men.

When institutions drastically fail to provide and do severe damage as by brutal exploitation unsuccessful war or incompetent tyranny people respond with political turmoil and aim at a revolution in government when conditions are or are also "dehumanizing" there is alienation anomie mental disease delinquency and generation gap and we come to the cultural and religious crisis that is the subject of this book my subject is the breakdown of belief and the emergence of new belief in sciences and professions education and civil legitimacy.

LADY IN RED these men friends of ours who smile nice stay unemployed and take us out to dinner LADY IN PURPLE lock the door behind you LADY IN BLUE wit fist in face to fuck LADY IN RED who make elaborate mediterranean dinners & let the art ensemble carry all ethical burdens while they invite a coupla friends over to have you are sufferin from latent rapist bravado & we are left wit the scars.

But we are the leaves we move like sunlight through the trees we strike as suddenly as the rain and our arrows are poisoned raindrops and then we are gone our Warriors become leaves once more and we are one with the Invisible soon even our women will be as green as flowers and no devil will ever be able to see them.

The formula for writing biographies of individual men and women has as we have seen been thoroughly worked out apart from the recent introduction of psychoanalytical methods and a little libido it has remained more or less the same since Plutarch but in writing the biography of a protoplasmic continuity like typhus it becomes necessary to develop a new formula.

The first precise and modern treatment of plane geometry was due to Hilbert 1862-1943 in his approach there were five undefined terms and fifteen postulates we shall not pursue this example any further except to emphasize that it does not matter at all what one *thinks of* when the undefined terms are used the important thing is that they have the properties given in the postulates.

Le Secrétaire d'Etat des Etats-Unis d'Amérique prie par les présentes toutes autorités compétentes de laisser passer le citoyen ou ressortissant des Etats-Unis titulaire du présent passeport sans délai ni difficulté et en cas de besoin de lui accorder toute aide et protection légitimes.

In his sixth year as the dictator of Germany Adolf Hitler was ready to grab the extra Lebensraum *living space that he had promised the Germans in 1938 he had annexed Austria and sealed the Munich Pact with Britain and France which awarded the Sudetenland area of Czechoslovakia the Pact guaranteed the new boundaries of the rest of Czechoslovakia but in March 1939 Hitler violated the Pact and seized the rest of the country in a swift bloodless takeover this was followed by the annexation of the Baltic port of Memel and the Free City of Danzig then after protecting himself against Russian interference by signing a nonaggression pact with Stalin Hitler sent his troops marching into Poland and set off World War II.*

Dunkers in all-night diners cabbies dozing on the hack lines night watchmen charwomen lighthouse keepers and all the others standing the great night watch in Manhattan and along the eastern seaboard have one companion that never goes to sleep on them that cheerful stayer-up is WNEW's Milkman's Matinee a 2-to-7 a.m. program of recordings small-fry commercials and chummy gab conducted six mornings a week by a young announcer named Stan Shaw your very good friend the Milkman and anxious parents like to have Stan broadcast his all-is-forgiven patter to runaways to date he has brought back 17.

Artistic crafts are now hardly more than luxuries occasionally supported by the state or by generous Maecenas they no longer supply language with those racy words and turns of speech which have been replaced by the bizarre or revoltingly abstract terms inflicted on us every day by politics and technology it is not poetry alone which is endangered the very integrity of the mind is at stake for all these words of our day all these abstractions of an inferior quality since they are not defined are content with a crumbling logic.

According to the general theory of relativity the metrical character curvature of the four-dimensional spact-time continuum is defined at every point by the matter at that point and the state of that matter therefore on account of the lack of uniformity in the distribution of matter the metrical structure of this continuum must necessarily be extremely complicated but if we are concerned with the structure only on a large scale we may represent matter to ourselves as being uniformly distributed over enormous spaces so that its density of distribution is a variable function which varies extremely slowly thus our procedure will somewhat resemble that of the geodesists who by means of an ellipsoid approximate to the shape of the earth's surface which on a small scale is extremely complicated.

To those who run the future there's always a better goat a better nerve gas producing confusion narcosis paralysis blindness some incapacitate a foe by casting him into a dream world of depression or witless euphoria mosquitoes infested with yellow fever and malaria fleas infected with plague ticks with tularemia relapsing fever and Colorado fever horseflies with cholera and anthrax dysentery they manipulate temperatures shooting material into the upper atmosphere thus lowering the temperature below interrupt the heat being radiated from earth thus raising the earth's temperature and set off explosions on the continental shelf causing tidal waves and earthquakes or target continents for catastrophic rains I play utterly abstract music on a bass kazoo *what ought what ought what ought I do?*

Today on the contrary books are in great abundance and variety available at any place whatsoever not only to Ptolemaic kings but also to any private individual and at a moderate cost however I am afraid that the abundance and cheapness of books may cause us to become less industrious we may be like banqueters who being surfeited with gorgeous and sumptuous dinners wave away ordinary and nourishing food and prefer to stuff themselves with elaborately prepared but less healthy repasts.

This is why I could not approve of all of those trouble-making and quarrelsome types who called neither by birth nor by fortune to manage public affairs never cease in their imagination to effect some new reformation and if I thought there were the slightest thing in this essay by means of which one might suspect me of such folly I would be very sorry to permit its publication my plan has never been more than to try to reform my own thoughts and to build upon a foundation which is completely my own and if my work having sufficiently pleased me I show it to you here as a model it is not for that reason that I wish to advise anyone to imitate it.

Suburbia defined as an ideology a faith in communities of limited size and a belief in the conditions of intimacy is quite real the dominance of the old values explains more about the people and the politics of the suburbs than any other interpretation fundamentally it explains the nature of the American metropolis it indicates why our large urban complexes are built as they are why their inhabitants live the way they do and why public programs are carried out the way they are if these values were not dominant it would be quite possible to conceive of a single gigantic metropolitan region under one government and socially conscious of itself as one community the new social ethic the rise of the large organization would lead us to expect this development as a natural one the automobile the subway the telephone the power line certainly make it technically possible they even push us in this direction but the American metropolis is not constructed in such a way it sets its face directly against modernity those who wish to rebuild the American city who protest the shapeless urban sprawl who find some value in the organizational skills of modern society must recognize the potency of the ideology until these beliefs have been accommodated reform will not come in the metropolitan areas nor will men buckle down to the task of directing in a manner consonant with freedom the great political and social organizations on which the nation's strength depends a theory of communication and a theory of local government are at odds with the prerequisites of contemporary life and so far theory has been the crucial force that preserves the suburb there is no economic reason for its existence and there is no technological basis for its support there is only the stubborn conviction of the majority of suburbanites that it ought to exist even though it plays havoc with both the life and government of our urban age.

Last May the White House released a list of 22 "critical" technologies orgnanized into six general categories materials manufacturing information & communications biotechnology & life science aeronautics & surface transportation and energy & environment the list stongly emphasizes materials technologies followed by information and communications although relatively low on this list applied molecular biology and medical technology were nevertheless mentioned.

This woozy funambulist syntactic
reflexes all atwitter had patterned
his pat patter after acrobatics
born of conventional learned and learned
wisdom but his motherly tongue willy-
nilly rendered such mimetic matter
higgledy-piggledy a real dilly
wrought of his proclivity to chatter
in risibly paronymous chit-chat
and aimless catachreses or rather
shameless catachreses a tightwire act
performed atop precarious blather
If words could catch the sense his lips let fall
one might observe he made no sense at all.

mumble the
words you understand call them
four brothers strain to catch the sense
but have to admit it's
in a language
they've not taught you
a flaw somewhere
and for answer well
that
long unbroken line
of the hills
there

High o'er the roof of the world he soars free and unfettered as the roaring wind itself behold the sky-born spanner of a trillion galaxies the restless streaking stranger from the farthest reach of space this glistening gleaming seeker of truth whom man shall call forevermore *The* **SILVER SURFER!**

We'll just have to face it that when Boris Karloff goes we've had it we'll have lost our beloved best of modern times we'll be sunk I hope these words come to your attention Mr. Karloff in the best of health and that the remaining years of your life are a great source of pleasure & satisfaction to you.

5 If you miss a pill it should be taken as soon as remembered if you miss two pills they should both be taken as soon as remembered take the next pill at the usual time there is a chance of becoming pregnant if you miss only one or two brown white or light-yellow pills and that chance increases with each successive day that a scheduled brown white or light-yellow pill is missed any time you miss one or two pills except the light-green inactive pills you should also use another method of birth control until you have taken a brown white or light-yellow pill daily for 7 consecutive days if you miss one or more light-green inactive pills you are still protected against pregnancy *provided* you begin taking your brown pills again on the proper day.

The patient is well hydrated to assure a full bladder and the foreskin is fully retracted to prevent washings from the prepuce from contaminating the specimen the glans penis is cleansed with an antiseptic solution the patient voids and the first voided 10 ml of urine are collected for a urethral culture the patient voids about 200 ml and a midstream aliquot is obtained for a bladder specimen the patient then bends forward and continues to retract the foreskin the physician massages the prostate gland and collects drops of expressed prostatic fluid for prostatic culture.

Be fruitful and multiply and fill the earth the fear of you and the dread of you shall be upon every beast of the earth and upon every bird of the air upon everything that creeps on the ground and all the fish of the sea into your hand they are delivered every moving thing that lives shall be food for you and as I gave you the green plants I give you everything only you shall not eat flesh with its life that is its blood for your lifeblood I will surely require a reckoning of every beast I will require it and of man of every man's brother I will require the life of man whoever sheds the blood of man by man shall his blood be shed for God made man in his own image and you be fruitful and mutiply bring forth abundantly on the earth and multiply in it.

At the south coast hook of land that curls east to west there are some lovely beaches at Les Salines most of them are empty during the week although the ones reached by paved road are enjoyed by Martiniquais and others on weekends those reached by dirt road are almost always reasonably underpopulated.

The difficulty of discovery in the close world which the human is because it is ourselves and nothing outside us like the other is that definition is as much a part of the act as is sensation itself in this sense that life *is* preoccupation with itself that conjecture about it is as much of it as its coming at us its going on in other words we are ourselves both the instrument of discovery and the instrument of definition.

Stein's theme is writing but in such a way as to be writing envisioned as the first concern of the moment dragging behind it a dead weight of logical burdens among them a dead criticism which broken through might be a gap by which endless other enterprises of the understanding should issue for refreshment it is a revolution of some proportions that is contemplated the exact nature of which may be no more than sketched here but whose basis is humanity in a relationship with literature hitherto little contemplated and at the same time it is a general attack on the scholastic viewpoint that medieval remnant with whose effects from generation to generation literature has been infested to its lasting detriment it is a break-away from that paralyzing vulgarity of logic for which the habits of science and philosophy coming over into literature where they do not belong are to blame.

Space is not an empirical concept which has been derived from outer experiences for in order that certain experiences be referred to something outside me that is to something in another region of space from that in which I find myself and similarly in order that I may be able to represent them as outside and alongside one another and accordingly as not only different but as in different places the representation of space must be presupposed the representation of space cannot therefore be empirically obtained from the relations of outer appearance on the contrary this outer experience is itself possible at all only through that representation.

Let me insert here a parenthetical remark. I mean it when I speak of male writing. I maintain unequivocally that there is such a thing as *marked* writing that until now far more extensively and repressively than is ever suspected or admitted writing has been run by a libidinal and cultural hence political typically masculine economy that this is a locus where the repression of women has been perpetuated over and over more or less consciously and in a manner that's frightening since it's often hidden or adorned with the mystifying charms of fiction that this locus has grossly exaggerated all the signs of sexual opposition and not sexual difference where woman has never *her* turn to speak this being all the more serious and unpardonable in that writing is precisely *the very possibility of change* the space that can serve as a springboard for subversive thought the precursory movement of a transformation of social and cultural structures.

A theory which should be capable of being absolutely demonstrated in its entirety by future events would be no scientific theory but a mere piece of fortune telling on the other hand a theory which goes beyond what may be verified to any degree of approximation by future discoveries is in so far metaphysical gabble.

The concept of the historical progress of mankind cannot be sundered from the concept of its progression through a homogeneous empty time hence a critique of the concept of such a progression must be the basis of any criticism of the concept of progress itself.

This glossary includes words commonly confused such as accept and except words commonly misused such as hopefully and words that are nonstandard such as hisself it also lists colloquialisms and jargon colloquialisms are expressions that may be appropriate in informal speech but are inappropriate in formal writing jargon is needlessly technical or pretentious language that is inappropriate in most contexts.

He needs without knowing those old Renaissance formulas equating C-sharp minor with longing sudden modulation to E major with a glimpse of heaven how dare an obnoxious greaser four years younger than he turn the Civil War tune "Aura Lee" into the Hit Parade standard "Love me Tender" without a wiggle of concern for the underpinning chordal message either this language *has no content* or tonal tastes have festered fixed for 100 years and more both options terrify him.

Funny day looking for laughter and finding it there sunny day braiding wild flowers and leaves in my hair picked up a pencil and wrote "I love you" in my finest hand wanted to send it but I don't know where I stand telephone even the sound of your voice is still new all alone in California and talking to you and feeling too foolish and strange to say the words I had planned I guess it's too early 'cause I don't know where I stand crickets call courting their ladies in star-dappled green thickets tall until the morning comes up like a dream all muted and misty so drowsy now I'll take what sleep I can I know that I miss you but I don't know where I stand I know that I miss you but I don't know where I stand.

There is a saying *Cambian sempre come la salsa* always changing like sauce because the variety of sauces is so great pasta is eaten with every kind of vegetable eggplant zucchini zucchini blossoms and leaves artichoke hearts cauliflower broccoli fava beans peas potatoes lentils beans chickpeas and chestnuts and also with chicken livers meatballs bits of pancetta and sausage *pasta 'ncasciata* in a mold consists of layers of macaroni fried chicken livers meatballs sliced eggplant tomato pulp bits of salami basil with grated cheese and eggs to bind it all into shape real baroque cooking but most pasta dishes are incredibly simple examples of just how attractive *cucina povera* can be peasants fed themselves entirely on pasta so it had to be good and they put in what they could typical sauces are made not just with the many vegetables but also with seafood cuttlefish and their ink clams mussels and shrimp and newborn fish so small they look like a lump of jelly these can be sardines red mullet and other fish fishing for them is forbidden most of the year the fishermen use special nets but they always seem to be around.

But a central organ of information and instruction for all the localities would be equally valuable in all departments of administration a government cannot have too much of the kind of activity which does not impede but aids and stimulates individual exertion and development the mischief begins when instead of calling forth the activity and powers of individuals and bodies it substitutes its own activity for theirs when instead of informing advising and upon occasion denouncing it makes them work in fetters or bids them stand aside and does their work instead of them the worth of a State in the long run is the worth of the individuals composing it and a State which postpones the interests of *their* mental expansion and elevation to a little more of administrative skill or of that semblance of it which practice gives in the details of business a State which dwarfs its men in order that they may be more docile instruments in its hands even for beneficial purposes will find that with small men no great thing can really be accomplished and that the perfection of machinery to which it has sacrificed everything will in the end avail it nothing for want of the vital power which in order that the machine might work more smoothly it has preferred to banish and the First Amendment says Congress shall make no law respecting an establishment of religion or prohibiting the free exercise thereof or abridging the freedom of speech or of the press or the right of the people peaceably to assemble and to petition the Government for redress of grievances and one way of understanding ergonomics is to think of the body as a machine with thousands of moving parts like any machine the parts have limited capacity push a part too hard or ask it to perform outside of its design specifications and the potential for reduced performance even breakdown is heightened as this sort of travel creates its own peculiar type of event and innervation so it also has its own special form of fatigue like a fibrillation of muscles striated by the excess of heat and speed by the excess of things seen or read of places passed through and forgotten the defibrillation of the body overloaded with empty signs functional gestures the blinding brilliance of the sky and

somnambulistic distances is a very slow process things suddenly become
lighter as culture our culture becomes more rarefied and this spectral form of
civilization which the Americans have invented an ephemeral form so close
to vanishing point suddenly seems the best adapted to the probability the
probability only of the life that lies in store for us the form that dominates the
American West and doubtless all of American culture is a seismic form a
fractal interstitial culture born of a rift with the Old World a tactile fragile
mobile superficial culture you have to follow its own rules to grasp how it
works seismic shifting soft technologies and technology by its nature
embodies a denial of continuity an escape from history in its ability to each
time do anew so it is more than ever left to the new teacher in her role as
communicator to provide continuity for we are left with what we can pass on
a way of doing things history embodied in technology and this has ever been
the case but it is only in this self-consciously technological age that we see our
way of doing things and our history so clearly embodied in machines so
expensive that we hardly believe ourselves when we call them tools the voice
from the telescreen was still pouring forth its tale of prisoners and booty and
slaughter but the shouting outside had died down a little the waiters were
turning back to their work one of them approached with the gin bottle
Winston sitting in a blissful dream paid no attention as his glass was filled up
he was not running or cheering any longer he was back in the Ministry of
Love with everything forgiven his soul white as snow I am forgetting the
erasure the disturbance the intent the sale the kinship the sharing the
comrade the dog the traffic this awakening misappropriation situated
between its pronoun and personal possession how it came about it is coming
it rewards comeuppance with forgetting it has it has had a whole background
that birds parts and wholes and are taken apart how the objects situate the
human is not a question which is not but has been were and might fever a
fervent future adventure or woman but further and if planetary thinking
requires that we embody the realization of groundlessness in a scientific
culture planetary building requires the embodiment of concern for the other
with whom we enact a world my darling since you and i are thoroughly
haunted by what neither is any echo of dream nor any flowering of any echo
but the echo of the flower of dreaming somewhere behind us always trying
or sometimes trying under us to is it find somehow but O gracefully a we
entirely whose least breathing may surprise ourselves let's then despise what
is not courage my darling for only Nobody knows where truth grows why
birds fly and especially who the moon is Season's Greetings with love famous
last words tazmanian speed zone ahead encrypting my signature my
handshake my spectacled body the meat of the argument loss of a hand or a
foot shall mean severance at or above the wrist or ankle joint but only on
condition that the body and through it nature should first be posited in the
experience of an irreducible spatiality So Rose did not sing but she had to do
something and my cyclone soul has grown deep like the rivers

Your exploration of the networks will eventually take you to facilities of other campuses and institutions where you will meet quite different operating systems policies and attitudes toward networked computing a library that is there today may be gone tomorrow essential commands may be different a trick that worked yesterday may not work today it is best to develop self sufficiency and resilience while networking and yet maintain contact with consultants to be aware of and to communicate change.

And a final bootleg to wit when it is recognized that the symbolic system of poetry resides in the mechanisms of thought in certain procedures or formulations independent of language yet contained within it often transcending it or negating it as common sense then the time will be ripe for determining the complex system to which poetry is bound in the scheme of knowledge and of the continual becoming of beings and things which is alright as far as it goes but don't hold your breath life is an occasion for poetry which is to say poetry is an expression of life an occasion to assert the signal importcane of langauge as contsitutive of the wold hot-damn! I only wish the guy were here to debate it with me I bet he could give me a difficult time like those other folks I've hybridized or bastardized as some will no doubt have it but I'll hold to a few claims in any case one that you're getting tired of me two that I'm getting tired of myself three that there is more to life than great conversation and four that great conversation is something what the hell not a thing to aspire to just the same a bit of incentive a roundtable a conference meeting as Allen had it of minds and as that comedian had it a flagrantly pithy common carrier chock-full of macaronic.

And those of you who are living and\or alive and are so (pre)disposed against the foregoing modified juxtaimpositional anthology are entitled of course to sue my ass no hard feelings it's a free bitmapped country and guess what? it don't add up and you know what? I told you so.

17

NOTES

& it's personal ethos obliges me to thank the following individuals & please
NOTE institutions be damned mine included permission by birthright is founding poetic principle

W. J. King
A. C. Bhaktivedanta Swami Prabhupada
Avital Ronell
E. M. Wn.
Herman Melville
Wallace Stevens
Walter Kent and Walton Farrar
J. W. N. Sullivan
Maxwell Grant
Ezra Pound
Mary Daly
Paul Goodman
ntozake shange
Dennis J. Reardon
Hans Zinsser
Neal H. McCoy
Paul Valéry
Albert Einstein
Don Byrd
Giambattista Vico
René Descartes
Robert C. Wood
Jamie Dinkelacker
Stan Lee and John Buscema
Forrest J. Ackerman
Margaret Zellers
Charles Olson
William Carlos Williams
Immanuel Kant
Hélène Cixous
Charles Sanders Peirce
Walter Benjamin
Diana Hacker
Richard Powers
Joni Mitchell
Claudia Roden
John Stuart Mill
Jean Baudrillard
Michael Joyce
George Orwell
Abigail Child
Francisco J. Varela, Evan Thompson, and Eleanor Rosch
e. e. cummings
Hakim Bey
Michel Foucault
Gertrude Stein
Langston Hughes
Mike Randal
Tristan Tzara
& Derek Owens & Greg Hewett & Jody Swilky & Eleni Varsamidou & Stuart Moulthrop &
Martin Rosenberg, you're all in this someplace somehow

Anatomy of a Body

a

Academy of Pop:
A Critical Essay
in Four Parts
with Instructions
Reproduced Here
for Your Viewing Pleasure

[& edited by J. Armstrong
Williams.—Ed.]

12 March 1991, or
some time ago ...

nd yes, people
extraordinary
moments, bringing
ordinary things:
few of these lay
kree-'churz

      gathered
together, presumably

      to exchange a
few ideas, experiences perhaps
hoping, ultimately
     to make it with one
another, a truly

    dialogic teleology
     personified by yours
truly. What's that
you say?
     This is
     to be
scrutinized, closely, checked
and rechecked to ascertain

to ascertain what? What's your
model, your game, your
    name? Do I know
you, do I
know you? Should I
know you? Do you
     know me?
Would you like to?
Really?
    Not really?

Are you certain?
   Are we

in a room?

on this planet?

Am I
here and
there?

And
tomorrow?
What is the basis for
this
conversation this
conflict
of interest this
mediation these
er this construction
project this this
event?
n   o cca si on sit e sit u ati
on pfu z zy an din disc rim in ate

in itself
and that's it
huh? That's what this
is this is this.............
rformer's text................sten,
b...and...............Huh?.......yeah..........
,........
.........o.k......so-and-soso vita......x,
change-of-p[l?—Ed.]
ace:...........rdsciencesel...
....xwork?...
..[gargled in fax l trans   missions-
-Et.]

I'm inclined to believe
what you tell me, provided you are
well inform'd, well
meaning, meaning
me no harm. Or provided you you
are well
provided
for know
what we're talking and I'm
writing and you're reading

about. If not, just sit there and
shutup
shutup and laugh
I dare you—
[Again...Ed.]
—therapeutically

let's just say
I, poker face and all, do (know
what I'm etc.).
Married for a few moments, then, a
few
fleeting
fucking
moments------
The canon: an
invention, a mystification, a
political situation
comedy, something for all and each
to worry about
after dinner.
Earlier
this morning, pancakes, juice

the earth was flat, no
oyster.
Canon
formation
or its plural as
aesthetic dilemma
or its plural:
I don't
like my eggs
undercooked. I hate
god.

Of course a course
may consist a anyting, anyting
at all, just name y\our centricity:

Musicology 272: I
Want to Change the World, or
The Social Construction
of Electric Guitar Solos.

c

Batman 101: Bob Kane's
Dream of a Postapocalyptic
Chiropteran Polis, Guano and All.

Women's
Studies 300: Interrelations, or,
Postmodern Makeup, Mothers of
Invention and
the Animal Rights Movement.

Technical Writing 252: How to
Teach Something
That Doesn't Really Exist.

Physics 10^9: What Are Black
Holes, and
Why Are They Saying These Crazy
Things About Us?

and thus we cross disciplines,
Q.E.D. ("We leave it to the ether to show...
but do we cross ideologies?
Wanna laugh, or is it that you
don't wanna
hurt my feelings?   (or is it
that Monty Python has
spoiled you? . . . .)

A question (?) to which I will
return some pixels hence, albeit
with a bit more t act.   (How do I
know these things
in advance?)

I could dance circles around you
if I could dance
and I'm no fascist
but aspire to be
better and keep right on talking
breathing, just look at me
this pitiful translation
in living color
I hurt.

I hurt, sneeze
fall into very pragmatic
luv [Or perhaps "ʟuʋu."—Ed.], stub
my
very pragmatic
toe, too.
                    Yes, mine
public, here to do with
what I want
                    a witty white
male, immodest, if I may say so
het (I think), single (for the
moment, sort of), euroamerican
(uh-huh)
middleclass, or so I'm told
institutionalized, like it or no
All as is the fashion, as
you like it
and after no fashion
in particular
likes   Molson Golden
anchovies on his pizza
          poetry, god knows why
Silver Surfer
          Jane's Addiction
the incredible versatility of
          Vaseline Petroleum
Jelly, god knows why
and
          yep, The Adventures
of Robin Hood.

          And sees real problems with
academic discurse
          despite a glimmer of hope
here and
there the focus on body,
say/write/or only read—the old
corpus, now incarnate—and
poiesis, but, shit, I'm supposed to
be a p-p-poet and, well
          my co nc er ns r

1 — Why print, and why not? (and
why write, and why repro—)
&
2 — Why continue to publish, and
why not?
&
3 -- How many cultures are we &
how nutritious are our media?

These ARE important
considerations for some of us.

Esp. me.   Really.

Mine students love me, anyway
I, them
me, us, them, we, ours, theirs
students, that is, people. We could
might have sex
with them—regularly, I think—
were it not for an ethically
rhythmic commitment
to what?
            Professorial
professionalism, role ["o"
w/circumflex?—Ed.], rules
        equanimity, fairness, grades
                privation, power
promotion.
            And, uv coarse
the fact that not all
of us are all
that disinterested
or discrete.   (Nevertheless it does
happen, a tacit
tempting grammar or
literacy.)
Anyway,   HEY!
You've got to hide
your love away, so
        it's not a question
of right and wrong
but of rights   and right
of Left and left of Right
and wrongs and

>>> **NO FRATERNIZING WITH
THE NATIVES!**   The signs are
everywhere. No
apologia, more
Areopagitica, good
and bad boys and girls
who just wanna be
boys and girls, poets
who just wanna critics who
just wanna be p-poets
like myself.   Let's call the whole
thing
off & on. We get paid to
get paid to
get paid to
get paid..

I endow you with the power ($) to
walk across the quad to that
building over yonder. You take the
opportunity. You return.
We are no longer in love.

Are my choices derived from
native ability? proximity?
influence? need? desire?
social experience? social
circumstance? forgetfulness?
        and what of 3rd. order
partial differential equations?
ethnicities? families?
equal opportunities? overtures?
the seven seas?

Ah, the sea:
                I could live
happily ever after
with this
somewhat-less-than-thick-
somewhat-less-than-random
description?....

Words SPEAK (to cop a phrase)
louder than actions.
And how many times hath I been
overheard   eth

by the global surveillance network
uttering (with calculator in one
hand and
large glass of Grade A
homogenized milk in other):

My discipline is a pain
in the class. My 1marxist2
feminist3deconstructive4pragmatic
s are a pain in the ass. My
knowledge, lewdick to a fault
worries me. My ideological
apparatus is creaky. I have a
headache. My sneaks are
too tight. They were manufactured
in the U.S. of A. I used to live in a
rundown,
old, second story---

but then, this is getting a bit TOO
personal....

and what happened to the
interrogative?

      Let's just say, all of us
                              I
hope to live happily ever after
condoms, condos
and those ever-popular 4 C
words—
cut, color, clarity, carat &
all.

      Have I sufficiently theorized
my
s elf?
                      a question I
hath ponder'd long and hard
after making love.
Primordially speaking, I think
mine answer has to do with
your answer.

I envision/empower my self
hovering around in my hot air
discurse balloon
trying to   identify   patterns
below   that function
independently of the
technologies   that set me
afloat. Aha—a man with a pipe
and a baseball cap
a ripe target for multicultural
study....
and I never quite make it back
to Kansas....

books are books, finally, stories are
stories
Mr. Knowledge is as Mr.
Knowledge does
he/me/she\it emerges out of an
impoverished ferment that owes as
much to
hellbent initiative as to
class-constrained or gender-based
or psychologically-motivated
or historically discursive
or ecologically imperative
constructs of desire, power, greedy
hege monies
the brewing industry.

Erratum: For "initiative" read
"enthusiasm." There is a wee bit of
induction, either
way....

              Yes, I, too, am against totaliz
er totalitarian theories
but each has the distinct benefit of

re cognizing the Other
by exclusion, omission,
counterexample....

And I do believe we may l/earn
something, then
from one an other—

f

                    how to be
productively hybrid, for example
how to refinish a piece of furniture
how to walk and
chew gum
how to be an
amat
eur
how to metabolize
institutions.
                    What wisdom
is this
is wisdom?

Hence the question before us (i.e.,
just you and me, babe)
at this moment:

        Do I have a voice? Do I have
many voices?

I lost my voice (i.e., mine).
                    Where?
Up in the hills
            somewhere,
listening to
Wynton.
            Found it
though, a bit
beatup and worn, still
                alwrite
political/emotive as
hell.
Don't believe me,   I don't
care.
Just ask me   and I'll show it
to you.
Anytime.
And if that's not   good
enough
then that's not
            good enough.
That's show biz.
Take my joke
                puh-leez.
And my voice.

Take my voice---
Just try and
take my voice and

I shall locate a new one....

            ---Unauthorized duplication
is a violation of applicable laws---
            (this is a limited time offer)

And am I that I am a man, heh
who likes talking
to those
who like to talk, heh, heh?
And is it true, what
the old timer told me, that
you can't teach poetry, that
poeta nascitur, non fit?

It might have something to do
with democracy.
It may have something to do with
democracy.
It surely has something to do with
democracy.
It has to do with democracy.
It is democracy.
It is democratic.   (mo/democratic?)
It is not democratic.

The tyranny of voices, finally, the
tyranny of the
reified self, the tyranny of many
reified selfs (i.e., The Tradition)
and what of the tyranny
of tyrants?
It begins here, with this page
[Right.—Ed.], and yet, and yet---
I need to speak, forcefully and with
abandon abandoning coercion and
hoping to
persuade
through the sheer generosity of my
appeal:
                I need you
        ?

Too strong, perhaps, yet   and permits
it is so.   this
                                                discurse

We cloak ourselves in exquisite
eloquences   about people and
        fancy formulae   things.
and
        all I hear is
                                a
predictably unpredictable
silence
                and I could cry

deathdeathdeath

        back, back to the cradle

                        I want to
                smell the corpse

corpus and all
                        I want to
know

        authentically
knowing knowledge

        is what got me, us
                        here here
and there

                for I may liberate the
text

                but liberation?

  The Motorola 68030

has made such a

        customer of me

Part 2 of 4

I see now that to re-see it is simply
insufficient, never was
and necessarily so.

To revise is to revisit, the cognate
has it
as ever
and I see now that sight requires
other modes of inquiry
to be site
                    this very oration
invoking
visitation rites and
or cognitive breaches, even

            paying one's   respects.
To see or not to see
but
ah, the sea, the sea, etc. etc.
The university   the Whole

            caverns measureless to
men, women
but let us not make too much
of our sources
etymologies.   I can smell,
touch, taste, hear
this scene, men
and women, naked, together, with
me---

            the ebb and flow of garbage
trucks
carrying our refuse
to the
            landfill. 'Tis an interesting
collection, more interesting ever
even than those magnificent
libraries
            we used to keep hearing
about.

Think a bit about the bulk of

manuscript drafts and memos
ushering forth from the desks of
the mightily educated
to commingle with the lowly
grocery lists
and Campbell's soup cans
and disk error floppies
and strangely pointed initiatives of
duh reel wOild:

Andy Warhol would be proud
maybe
but who does
he think
he was, anyway?
An   aesthetics of recycling
xplains the wonderful economy of
cultural artifacts
ashes to ashes, dust to dust
quid pro quo and
quid pro quo and
thaumaturgists of the critical
enterprise (there's no
faith like it)
fearing such
xposure
once propagated their own
desperate
historiopornography
(or so The Story, my diaversion,
goes):

to investigate the means and ends,
                    hows and whats of
        Whose Whos (? ?), that same old
                            same old
of googolplex goodoleboy bonding
                    meanwhile shunning
the whys and whens and wheres of
such.....postcolonial, imperialist
                            tekhnes
                    themselves recycling
only to paraphrase, para   doxic ally
                    a few ancient tropes
            in an effort to immortalize that
                    which must, it must

be admitted, come
only to pass....

(It might comfort youse to know
that many of these folks are
currently enjoying a somewhat
foreign
habitat)

....in all, nice work
if you can get it, & haven't I
dropped all appropriate indicators?
Is this
what I'm about, too? Is this
what I intend? Will I
endure, even after
the end?.....
(the easy way
out.)
BUT—and I
autoplagiarize here, so to speak
when I write, saying aloud
to my   self

W e
may be armed with
too much theory
to engage in meaningful combat.

That is:
well, it's already been
writ, hasn't it.   [Rhetorical.—Ed.]

I must confess, mom and dad
I grow weary of ontologies
masquerading as reflexive
epistemologies, and
vice-versa .... besides, I'll watch you
die
if it all works the way it's supposed
to.

Is it just me, or am I being
too hard on ourselves?

—I begin to resist my
resistance, for I, too
have family photo albums
glossy snapshots from a past
in which I played no part
possessed no voice
now interject my
expansive and generous
ego
geocentrically, as before, but a
subspace, a territorialized
subspace, a collage here and there
my discurse
hoary and incontinent, my discurse
forgiven by me and me alone, its
moment, too, co ming, cunningly
to pass, so what am I so cussing and
pissing and moaning about?---

BUT can living matter
issue forth from non-living
matter, matter, in fact
that has never been alive?
A question seemingly answered
late
last century (cf. the biogenesis
debate, and recall J. H. Newman's
and G. Stein's conceptions of
"useful knowledge")
and reconstructed here
for your reconsideration, dear
fellow parasites.

End of frontier	1890
End of margin	1990

Yawn. Er—±%.
A n
echo: What were we?

well naturally, say you, *but there is*
ahem valuable work to be done
after all, my good cryonic reprobate
& .... or, perhaps you hold me in
contempt for my facile

approach
to the academy .... or, perhaps I
simply don't interest you. Fine. I
didn't invite you
here. But stay a while. You might
regret having come, after all.
        I'm not a bad cook,,,,,,,,
it's just that I plain refuse to
optimize, chocolate or vanilla...

We've all heard it all before, or
haven't we?

That is, if you think I have a
destination in mind, you're
wackier than me.
Kind only to be cruel, it would
seem
Judeo-Christian-ly speaking.

Where were we?
Are we hearing
the same language?

Haven't we "made"
                        "love"
"before"?

        appassionato?

Read any good books
lately?

" ... and we have an
unconfirmed report that
colonies of nomadic experts
each specializing in that
literacy peculiar to
        a specific letter of
the Roman alphabet
having just last month
declared themselves a viable
cultural subtext
are now demanding sanctuary
from holistic zeitgeist.
Stay tuned ... "

Yeah, o.k. And it's not that
like everything else
I'd forgotten. It's just that
I'd felt it
better to keep laughing through it
all, me, a most
nimble nomad, readymade
misread, unscrewed, wired
scanned and screened and targeted
        by most accounts
trying to concretize
a-b-s-t-r-a-c-t-i-o-n
trying to appropriate megananopop
                hodologies,

                met   trying too
hard
for mine own good, not to say
survival
revisingrevisingrevising....

And oyez oyez oh yeah

        "We just brought a whole new meaning
        to Pecan Sandies. Our new bite-size
                Pecan Sandies are
        miniature versions of the larger size
        with lots more fun. All the richness
        you've come to expect in a new smaller
                        size.
                One bite
                is all you'll need to fall
        for these delicious new cookies."

And yes, I'm not being evasive
for all the world, all the world's
a stage, game, set of conventions
conventional and otherwise
and—something more
than a {[Macintosh?] uni verse of
discurse}, but what?—
a driven CD-ROM jukebox
crapshoot exceptions
to prove our idiosyncracies
sensitivities
odors, fragilities

k

and if I write
well
will you know how to read me?
    and if I'm full of facts
will I still **bleed**?

I have walked across the quad
with you this time. It is unfriendly
here
the people all dress differently
and have steep foreheads. It was
to be expected
and we approach the object
approaching, perceiving,
measuring, describing, reading,
interpreting....

The object is an apple.

The object is a map.

The object is a tree.

The object is a mirror.

The object is a verb.

The object is a subject.

The object is an object the

        body is that of a 64
inch, 125 pound, Caucasion female,
who appears compatible with the
stated age of 67. The scalp has
brown hair with gray at the base.
The orbits are free of petechiae.
There is no acute bruising of the
mouth. An endotracheal tube is cut
off within the mouth. There is a
multilumen catheter inserted
beneath the midportion of the right
clavicle with multiple pinpoint
punctures about this area. There is
an intravenous line in each
antecubital fossae. There is a sub
xiphoid pinpoint puncture of the

skin. The abdomen is without acute
injury. The dorsal aspects of both
forearms show pinpoint punctures
compatible with venous access
sites. There is a urinary catheter.
The lower extremities are without
edema or scaling of the skin. The
back is without acute injury.

Heart: overall increase in
interstitial membranes of
lymphocytes and   plasma
cells. There are many minute
patches of myocyte loss
        with early fibroplastic
response and hemosiderin laden
        macrophages

Lung: black pigment in
lymphatics

Liver: fine droplet
vacuolization

Spleen: within normal limits

Gastrointestinal Tract:
        multinucleate cells in the
mucosal
        lymphoid aggregate

Pancreas: within normal limits

Adrenal: within normal limits

Kidney: minute subcapsular
cortical scars with obsolescent
        glomeruli

Thyroid: follicles are small with
relatively little colloid storage

hath seen it with
                with
thine own eyes
topical
        optical

elisions
        an essentialist's essentialism
working through the flimsy fibers

          amorphous plasmas

            neural nebulae
of lived
          and felt
experience
     and clearly a
constructed consciousness
indurate

constructing identity, or former
identity   [Flesh made
      word?—Ed.]

            perhaps
       to steal away your he
arts

       more at PLAGIARIZE
but

what is more? what is there left

       once red, well, healed

     and how
but many ways

woman, man, or child

a being who was
          being

       no less and
more
   than these

   obscene

    particles of flesh

and blood
          a touch of hope, say
type write
a dab
      of aspiration
            a sense of
taste?

Such a cold finger over
sleepy garden walls under
the Milky Way with a song in my
heart of aging children comes
a time people, people who need
someone to watch over the way
you look
as I wander down the lane and out
to the
ballpark, but we didn't start a fine
romance for every bear that ever
there was so
just set 'em up, joe, footloose and
fancy free to be caught in the rain
raspberryred lemonyellow
orangeorange . . .

          I wish I
could

         be
metaphysical

         carry
moonbeams
home in a jar . . .
       but I know, I
know
I'd have to stop, sooner or later.

And so do you.

Part 3 of 4

That I may have
designs on you
the ruse
I have operated under
parts, whole and
all
a gendered, genred
legibility
but a uuunit-y, a fffamily [In '95?
Ugh.—Ed.], a nnnetwork,
nnnodes?
                    Take your pix....

I am most comfortable
believing
you believe me, hard
and soft as that may be
to believe
my shape and substance
owing less to macroeconomic
expectations
less to Poesy
or critiquE
than to sheer disregard
for a few conventions.

What's to be made of this?
And what's to be done with this
hyperactive
bullshit artiste?

We live and die
aleatorically speaking
while in three or four dimensions
exhibiting something less than a
perpetual smile
but the mind's body
an organism ultimately
        can cook?   Not quite yet . . .
impossible to differentiate
from the mind

or from the body
        probe as one may
is stuck, at last, with the task
of making a few claims
as to what one is likely to confront
over a period of, say, write
        decades
however culturally, or socially
economically
or biologically specific
one may regard one's
ecosphere. One's.

There's nothing quite like a
surprise
options, possibilities, pleasant
and otherwise
and the day Homo sapien
is anaerobic and flameproof
may be that day
when we finally confront
the fluxing substance
the ways
we were....

it's not a plea for universals
in the old sense of that word
or world
but an intimation
of mortality   a
migration toward what we
        love
I'm after
a feeling, is all
that I, too, have become too
formal/funereal
whenever I hath smelled
something
new, that what I know is, well
known
a certain self-construction
of certainty
my feet, as I am wont to say
hitting the floor
each morning
when I arise....

[Aubade excised—Ed.]
            take a good look at
that $10 word
"interdisciplinarity" or its variants
and ask our self (yes, with a small
's')

What languages, what assumptions
are at work
to promote such
understanding?

And it's not habit
or habitude, finally
but something vaguely
anthropomorphic
perhaps the impulse behind
anthropomorphism
a thing worth resisting
but worth also, i think
a few words from our
corporate sponsors (e.g, Post
Raisin Bran, the fashion industry)
and a few words
of prayer
and a few
blasphemies, i tink you call 'em---

divorcedivorcedivorce

I am in a position
to address this latter category
for I find myself inf(l)ected
with the viruses of the times
unaesthetically speaking
and   none fatal, no, not yet
save   life, but some everlasting
and
        I resent it
and I
            do not resent it....This
is serious business, though it be not
serious.

I learned how to cook

                            during
hard times
my
            modest talents, in o-so-
vulgar
terms

                    a tribute to working
class
consciousness   [?—Ed.]
                            the
practical wisdom of
of

                practicemakesperfect.

No   good cook seeks
perfection
            of course
                            rather
a momentary satisfaction
                                    a
provisional satiation
with that which

                            itself transformed
transforms

living thoughts and deeds

                steeped in material
                        matters

            like oven temperatures

                            fluctuating

like wine
                        perishable ...

The cook knows her foodstuffs

                    analyzes her recipes
                        admires her
cheeses
and tomatoes

                sniffs for the
sake
of sniffing

                      taking
foolish pride in her
accomplishments

              flavors   to
taste

      personifies her pots

and pans and
              loves her work.

If transcendence
                      were
simply
the raison d'être
for raison d'être
      she could find it in a good
loaf of bread, even poor Plato's
pleasure
I'm sure . . . .

the virus having
recourse to me
takes its full course courses
through
persuading me as to its
sincerity
and I begin to discard
my past
replacing it
with a new one
assassinating a few gods
or authors
as is the rage
I begin
to understand
hard times
as opportunities
for the poor page

and the world
I learn
is a rose....

                well, maybe an
arborvitae.

Category mistakes
are merely categories mistaken
for affinities, truths
and—yes, truths

truths

a word
'tis true
I'd forgotten, I think
intentionally....

                  "not interesting"
"irrelevant"
        "facts nor truths"
                  "outmoded"
        "oh please"....

O.k. Have i anyting
anyting at all
tuh do wid duh trut
duh whole trut
'n nuttin but duh trut?

Can/swer: No, not unless
you mean
                  what you say,
that is
                  generic truth,
truths, truth as

                  pragmatic
proposition, truth

                  not past but
true

                  to
commiseration.

(Is it true, accidentally
you still want to live with me?)

Is truth a construct?

Is truth an ideology?

Is truth a logic?

Is truth an ontology?

Is truth a discourse?

Is truth evolutionary?

    The truth is truth is
all of the above, true, no matter
how tight the fit
contingent, yes
and yes, human, all-too-human
and yes, geotemporally-specific
and yes, suspect
and yes, obligatory   (well....)
and yes, factual
    (email is emotive ;-))
and yes, constrictive
and no, unavoidable, finally
and hardly
arbitrary.
                  My god. My
word. My ass. Mine
all mine)))
Our disciplines accept
                        except
          specific claims
substantive and otherwise
              as truth
and ideologies, in the most
generous sense of this word
tend toward centricities, centers
of study, of locally global
bonding, of questions asked
and questions permitted to be asked
         of answers given
and answers permitted to be given
        and communities

identify themselves in accordance
with such questions and answers
    and assumptions pertaining
               thereto
and truth, in the most generous
       sense of this word
         is ideological
and something we just can't do
          without.

I've always enjoyed the category
"Movies"
in Jeopardy
have taken great pleasure in
exposing false inferences
and heartily endorse accuracy
and precision
            and a good pair
of shoes
to the extent that these are yet
possible (i.e., within monetary
allocations for fiscal year 1996)....

I dropped Webster's International
Unabridged (approx. 15.2 lbs., I
think)
on my big toe. That bastard hurt
like hell, or, as Webster's would
have it, like
"1 a (1) a nether world in which
the dead continue to exist."
It would probably have hurt about
as much
had I been in Tokyo at the time
but it might have meant
something different....

A friend of mine, a waiter
advises me that more and more
people
are consuming the ubiquitous
parsley garnish
which prompts me to consider the
inflection
of collective taste by the ubiquitous
new world order...

Rumor has it
innocence
is making a comeback....
Oh well. Out with it (in natural
language, please).

If there is no one community, there
is likewise no community
of one
whatever mode you think you're
in.   It's a tough world
out there
and even tougher
when I write about it.   Our fingers
are killing us (i.e., just you and me
and them, babe).

"So what you're telling me," I said,
fork in hand, about to taste the
eggplant she had prepared the
evening prior, "what you're telling
me is that truth, though not fixed,
is nonetheless a function of our
processing of 'reality,' 'facts.'
Consciousness at a given moment
is an awareness of sensations as
though there were, for instance, a
one-to-one correspondence
between words and things, causes
and effects, regardless the degree to
which such behavior is accountable
in theoretically reflexive terms.
And different, even alien societies,
cultures—though perhaps
processing their data differently—
will doubtless determine their own
versions of 'truth'?"

"Something like that," she
responded, "provided we allow
that the mind may consist of a
bundle of contradictory disclosures,
therefore that consciousness is not
simply the self-representation of a
brain in flux, but of a fluctuating
symbolization of brain. Now

shutup and eat your eggplant. It's
getting cold."

[Editor's Note: I have determined
that the above dénouement was in
fact inspired by a little known
(formerly) East German poem
entitled, "Closing the book" (c.
1988; anonymous author). My
translation follows:]

Distributing my undivided
attention
        in parallel
        I've become a compendium
of my times.

Deconstruction is in actuality
a defense
        against the corruption of the
signified; hence
        as a technology of signifiers
it ultimately
        mounts an assault not
merely upon logos as Truth
        but upon logos as image
logos as Madison Avenue.

Ok, lurking around the
neighborhood
        the syntax buttered up to me
and I
        swallowed it. Gangs
mysteries and all.

A sign so rendered
designated by the multiplicity
        of its truths, its henceforth
multiple meanings serving
        to deny the exigencies of
commodification.

It consisted of people, friends
of mine
        maybe just acquaintances
yeah

ok. Whatever is said
between us, after the Wall
comes down.

Metaphoricity, as the endless
capacity for displacing
  one sign by another, losing
any grounding in
  a preemptive signifying
Truth-image.

You know you think you
know something I
  don't, but you couldn't
prove it to me, so go
  eat a tomato. On my screen.

The subject as a self
composed of signs thereby
  granted provisional freedom
from the arbitrary
  yet motivated nature of
signification.

We danced in a shithouse,
Ozar's
  and I'm getting gum on my
foot while
  you might have been
dancing together.

There is no unified subject
except as a play
  of signifiers; there is no
unified subject as
  transcendental signified.

No, I had a beer, in a green
bottle
  you know the kind, you
were there.

The construction of the self
an eighteen-point plot.

Prove it to me. Prove to me

that you're worth it, and I'll
stop
  playing foosball. Them too.

The self has a complex and
is in a state of complex
desire.

It came back home. He left.
Sort of.
  Quickly.
Caveat emptor, yknow.
  We let the weeds grow as
    high
  as the porch. My brother
knows a lot
  about the stuff. So do you,
  he wrote
  death is a mystification, and
  they died, she, he, both
of
  and now they're both
  buried out there
  somewhere, together, I don't
know why
  I love your ph   give m

  danced together, like I
th   I sd. That abbrev.
  was enough, is. I walked
  out, him having
  come back home. The blood
had finally vanished, has, having.

  So screw me and
  our vax, too. By the way
  that book you're binding

makes me nervous
  and now that we're   here
where we wanna be
  again, what do you say? For
old times' sake
  is all. No big deal. Only
please—use
  ink.

Part 4 of 4

instructions for reading
me, my text, a school of
schools, fish-eyed
knocked-down, dragged out
these few words and
yours, too, & instructions
for listening to
a final egotism:

I, a builder, have asked YOU, a
builder, to participate
in my activity
perhaps have not permitted
you enough
breathingsplace
perhaps
have closed off   a few corridors
due to lack of
time?
perhaps
have been a bit automacratic
demanding. . . .

perhaps not.   We've all worked
under the table
kissed many a stranger
incurred multiple liabilities
lost a limb or two enjoyed
                    [Cf. Whitman.—
Ed.]
cheap thrills together, haven't we?
I like my constructions, they're
built to hold
more than two of each
and are, I might add
relatively inexpensive
but they are not foolproof
as evidenced by my innocent
complicity
my presence
my presentation
my news.

Representations were a form
of absence, naturally
and I've ground what axes I could
buried my hatchets
using the tools
of, I have a hunch, ontology. I do
believe, I do behave
differences, translations, images
aside
I do share
some things
in common
with Others, would be willing
to push that point
with them, myself
in atypically hegemonic terms
intent   —please
believe m— [Helvetica font.—Ed.]
on understanding my own
inadequacies, weaknesses
cracks in my foundation
        [Try SanFran font?—Ed.]
                    (PLUS two
women,
perhaps
y\o\ur objection, both real one
imagined).

No, never a retraction
                    simply a
moment rewrit a
reconciliation a

            reprise, begged
borrowed stolen
                unsolicited

        from what could well be a
favorite spaced
        out Martian. . . .

In short: I require your generosity
    ,,,have right along

and you, mine and
if we are to build this
          thing
together
we have to have faith
          careful, cautious
compromising, casual
faith
in something
ahead of us, a loose clause, say, a
bitmap, a bit of cause
an affect. . . .

a musing, m/Mosaic...

Pick your poison
as I've writ before
(and after)

the leftovers are all yours
metaphors tend to engineer
themselves

and try not to ground out
too quickly
for the stresses and strains are not
that
insignificant, media allows
and disallows, verse
comes and
goes and
kids like
us
learn
from our
compositional
efforts that what
comes out has gone in
and come out in more than one
or two ways:

          devic
     devic
like th
don
wor

as we
ere as
n the
reen

roll
tever
nd y're
iddng
rslf
f
ou
ink
u

on't
now
t...

re's
o
ision
ke
evision...

Hear and
understand
and
agree only
agree if you like.

Could it be
otherwise?

It's that
time
again
shaping
the deadline, you and me
from matter to
energy
the pixeled aye
and back to what
matters
w/o prayers
for letters, patented

u

or doctored, passing: this time
                                        of year

I will sleep at home, at home I   you'll find ME
hope one day to sleep.
Comes of practiced application, a   and my ASSOCIATES, my
hand mysterious to ease through   shadows
and mysterious this place once   committed
where once
could be and now, gone   and hungry
to seed gone.   as ever . . .

The street ends at the creek and the
creek
flows by the house the green house,
the cardboard
house that was there could have
been
there but now but now both
families perhaps have perished
or parts of that practiced application
of raising one thing or another
with a hand mysterious to ease
through

drifting up against or down the
creek, the waters
of that one year, 1972, tail-end of a
hurricane, departed
to wade up the street that ends at
the creek
through the waters

I dream, I sleep, I will sleep at
home, at home
I hope one day
to sleep ...

I'll be waiting at the far corner
                        of the quad
in many
cases
                where it is no
longer
green

and for those who have gone
or will go hungry . . .

AMATO'S
SICILIAN TOMATO SAUCE
with Meatballs

(approx. 4 quarts sauce)

Base (in a 10 in. omelette or *frying*
pan/skillet, medium-low h*eat*
uncovered):

 1 12 oz. can tomato *paste*
 (use Contadina brand, *if*
 possible)
 3-4 *medium-sized yellow*
 cooking *onions*
 6 cloves fresh *garlic*
 minced
 4 tablespoons o*live oil*
 1-2 teaspoons b*lack*
 pep*per*
 2 tablespoons basil (*fresh*
 and finely chopped, *if*
 possible)
 1 tablespoon finely
 chopped parsely (*use*
 cooking s*hears*)
 *1 cup sliced
 mushro*oms*
 *1/2 chopped *red*
 bell *pepper*
 *1/2 teas*poon*
 cayenne pepper
 *1 teaspoon
 oregano

Fry onions (with *optional*
*mushrooms, *bell pepper) in o*live*
oil until glassy and soft, add garlic *fry*
until *garlic just begins to change color*

Economics ties data base
for transformation of cultural materi
nutritional familial

ingredients of a lexicon personalized
know-how passed
along hand to
hand Spadafora
to Central New York lip to lip in
gestures from place

to place time
to time I gather my wits about
m e
to begin the
reenactment atop a stove (gas if
possible) a range of
energies and the rules vary
with what is lost in
translation not
and never mine alone the task
dynamic composed of
locale and
altitude and foodstuff product
brand or
climate with company and
loyalties in mind.
Here it is: read it, rework it
your way using your
options like me, my

Grandma would like

add rest of ingredients *(including
*cayenne, *oregano)*, fry until *paste*
separates with fork, dark burgundy *in*
color (approx. 45 minutes total).

In the meantime, cook in a separate *8*
qt. kettle, under medium heat *covered:*

    2 28 oz. cans (und*rained)*
    whole peeled *pear-shaped*
    tomatoes (quartered; use
    Red Pack brand, *if*
    possible, or equiva*lent*
    fresh tomatoes, pee*led)*
    1 28 oz. can *concentrated*
    crushed tomatoes *(use*
    Contadina brand, if
    possible)
    2/3 cup red wine (coo*king*
    wine ok)
    1 1/2 cups water
    1 tablespoon basil (dr*ied*
    o*k)*
    1 tablespoon *finely*
    chopped *parsely*
    plenty of black pep*per*
    salt (to taste as the sauce
    cooks)

When base is done, *add to kettle. Cook*
sauce covered at least 1 hour at
medium heat before adding meats
stirring every 10 minutes (it *should be*
gently boiling), spooning off any oil that
rises to surface. Add meats (see below) to
kettle, and simmer *covered*
for 2-3 hours longer, *stirring*
occasionally and again spooning off *oil*
from meats (add chicken, if desi*red only*
during last hour of cooking *to*
prevent separation from b*one).*
Refrigerate, reheat *slowly and simmer*
for one hour next day *for best flavor.*

*that and so would
Grandpa   Grandma & Grandpa's
tomato   sauce with   paste
    Grandma & Grandpa's
two   lines   here in this
hand-me-down recipe of
tried-and-true   technology and*

*I could eat boy I really could
eat but hers was oilier   more
pungent less   Americanized more
character almost
burnt.*

*We'd drink orange soda   being
kids and I liked the macaroni a little
hard with lots of freshly
grated cheese.*

*Grandpa would lean over and grate it
for me   Grandma would coax me
"Eat eat"
in Italian (we all know the
language) and I'd stuff myself*

to no end.

*There were arguments
indigestion   a residue
of hard times   long*

*before
and since and a light
salad anise cookies or grapes
after.*

Meatballs (approx. 20 *total):*

> 2 lbs. ground sirlo*in*
> 1 lb. ground pork (*put
> through grinder with*
> sirloin *only once)*
> 1 1/2 cups bread crumbs
> (Progresso brand *Italian*
> bread crumbs, or your
> own, *seasoned with salt*
> pepper, and parsely)
> 1 cup Romano (*or*
> Parmesan) cheese, grated
> *2 jumbo eggs*
> 3 cloves garlic, *minced*
> black pepper
> 2-3 tablespoons finely
> chopped parsely
> 1 teaspoon salt
> Dusting of *garlic powder*

Mix ingredients well. Each *meatball*
should be *round and slightly flattened.*
Fry in olive oil under medium heat
uncovered, until well browned, *all*
sides. Drain off oil and add to *kettle as*
above.

You may add 1-2lbs. (*sweet or hot)*
sausage, braciole, stew beef, *pork hocks,*
chicken parts, as *desired (all well-*
cooked and drained *prior to adding to*
sauce).

For vegetarian dishes, sauce *may be*
cooked as above *without the addition of*
meats (cooking *time remains constant).*

of macaroni   2
sausage links   1/2 loaf of
Italian bread   1 quart of
orange soda.
I couldn't move for a while   my
Grandma instructing me to wait a

while   then "Eat"   some

more   Grandpa laughing.

She could write her name, my

father's mother, Antoinette.
My Grandpa would ask me how man
senators in the Senate   how many
representatives in the   House.
When I said I didn't know   he'd
tell me   like I'm

telling you   but hunched over in
broken
dialect, my father's father's, Rosario'
I haven't been able to duplicate
her meatballs   the bread crumbs
she used perhaps the
secret   from a stale Columbus Bake
loaf   the best
in town.
I loved the bracioles   and pork
hockies, we called them.
We were all traditional
meat eaters.
My Grandpa once explained he came
to Syracuse because he was familiar

with the name.

I ate 10 once   2 plates

ANATOMY COSMIC

glue: **a monologue to be heard out & about**
              the neighborhood of somebody's virtual community

(ant ih   ero   ga in s   anti ge   n n   tibo dyag lutin ates
t hehe ro   ic: i   t'sa n e pic we 're aft   era sa ga
and after   who can say   but when?   but for the body as full a
abscents
as these [sigh] ns   poetically conceiv'd for a change
and

released: objctvst fashun had it (ended)   brace the line   r
lines
a concrete thng downntobjponents thena rose that
amsure
of measures   breath the line space the   energy
fields to
project   of amber   and then again   broke open
to the page and now   where?   these faiths
and the generosity   to inhabit the landscape   of an activity
of a
necessity   (no script ure, no)
that otherwise might not be   and what might
bring back togather   in spite of   writing   that is
creative
and when so much is a   being   writtenanent
with? possibilities may be imagined   tentative if torn
as under
reading?   or viewing?   to see|speak the place(s): or (all)
cnsmng:

yel   low: am i getting through?
closer . . . waiting   for a dancean age end a
for my bananas   yellowing   to yellow:

a culture long since having escaped   of casual departures
alphabetic villains having all
been all but   apprehended questioned
and re re leased   stories having been told   rel(eg)ated to
even at the genetic
or metaphorical level
recording and   too

                the attic of soul deserted

Z

```
wintered embryonic fatalities              of grammatical desire
where
we who store ourselves              victimless of musty odors
were we to pay our bills on time
what could we do but   to be?      but to do:
glue.
            gloo.
                    glue.glues
searching for what        in a word        sticks
to a place and this    unquestionably
unfashunable as        unfashunable as
nor unfathomable bonding
that "we" above  of the advocated and graphic
"I"   pixeled    shimmering            stor(i)ed

a mine for        and your        democracy

but to try a bit or two     harder takes some            tenderness
much as we who do       birthing        and die   class if   ied
do so                                   clueless:

(we might try    ssss inging it
bust a rap jack and jill
but not     here hear?      (of course not

there is this           something else                  not
business
again               swing Shift                         ing
a p(l)ace to slow down lie   linger alongside irregular margins or
missives or if you will     too quickly     and do you have an
uncle?

peed
      one
head
=     "to   make meaningful sense out   of"          somehow))

an old technics is what      past its prime   time
but of residual value                timing
```

AA

even amid chattering 0s and 1s   or among
talking   heads & tails:
(and pls. note: allallusions to demos graphics, koans and the like
are random & pre   medicated
elmer's is still the first
comes to mind
and they were singing it
with great enthusiasm
but in our view   these days
inefficiently:
                                    so we enhanced the original mono track
and man   it hums
esp. with fully digital processing
                if you care to give
a listen to w/o:
hence words speak   images   and these images
creating more of the same   which some
holding   scarred scared   to be sacred
resolved   whole:

must we always be talking   about him?   as though he were yet
alive?
must we?   and why not?
the thieves stole my   stereo
and I discovered just how   lost   we can be:
the need for static decompression unpacking   analog
corruption
of seemingly telempathic   noise   reveals
two tin cans fixed   (with a string   frayed   into which
seeps

(the rest of the world:

"i.e. it coheres all right
       even if my notes do not cohere." (((CXVI ...

          NOTE: Surfaces to be glued must be clean, dry, and free
                    of oil or grease.

PART ONE: THE APRICOT PRESERVE

Spreading across my tongue
a sweet tale
tasting of strong coffee
& toasted English muffin:

Two would-be siblings, one in Phoenix, the other in Cazenovia
who one day discover that the family business
run from afar by both thanks to modern networking technologies
(a jam & jelly concern, fruit picked in the San Joaquin
& pickled in Zanzibar
& famous for its apricot preserves)
is jeopardized by a bizarre development:

the labels will not stick to the corresponding jars.

That is, the strawberry labels will stick to the blueberry jars, &
vice versa
but no label will stick to its appropriate jar.

They boot up, pondering lucky stars & the like
connecting in spatialized space
the talky time of place
& begin to display peculiar anxieties
word-wise:

jar writes one, maybe a man
star writes the other, a woman
to most
afar write both
bizarre i add
& zanzibar
& we exhibit
to all prying eyes
trace qualities

of proximity
& anonymity &
entitlement
for we know something of each
other, & locales
& fear some of some reprisal
but we open up anyway
like the road
Route 89A northbound
from the Kaibab Plateau
across the wash
into southern Utah
by extension extending
moments of consciousness
& color flesh to
red to brown to beige
to red to white to
a grainy blue
across & around
spreading the words, w/o binding
like gospel, yes, nor mormon
but with desire to rupture
the continuum of longing:

this is one failure
the failure of resilience, conversion
into just about anything
& then again
the strength upon which
to begin to build
again
a sense of cohesion:

adhering then to violate
arbitration of properties
public & private

& motivations corresponding thereto
the motioning to and fro, disclosing
from speed limit to
limit
from ethical to aesthetic
& back again, protected
& no, the things to which
we grow attached
these & them
& to us
are to us
true
as Welles once said
of Cagney's acting:

the words w/syntax
connect & hold
surfaces to depths
or not
depending up-
on conviction
& the conditions
are not, nor have been
nor will be
nameless
nor does this obviate
the need
but that
the twists & turns
but to be driven
by the passions
of circumstance
must intersect with
anthropic contingencies
mortality, conflict, street brawls
the fact that

that we are of a piece
checkbook balance
or no
hat
or no
fingers on keyboard
w/pencil
or w/o:

(i might have some faith in you
he'd told them
if you knew why you were cheering
if only you knew
he sd
why structure
impresses you so):

all language the language
of sales, slogans
for lyrics lyrics
for slogans a radio, enveloping
for mood a mood
for purchase a purchase
become poetics a poetics
become evasion
(tax etc.):

        invasion
out of the question, then
by the foreign
when rendered familiar
by an international monetary exchange?

we're all
just one big
happy

famishing? ?a life   ?solely executed   ?needs be
camcorded . . .

o.k.

yet labels   "If *communication* had
affixed to product   several
meanings, and if
MUST be right   this plurality could
not be
as dictated by the jus, dharma   reduced, then
from the
of the marketplace, fair trade   outset it would
not be
practices, false   justified to define
advertising regulations, common   communication *itself*
as
human decency, common   the transmission of a
sense & the like   meaning
of like:

they conclude, somehow   assuming that we are
the labels would seem to be   capable of
understanding
intrinsically   one another as
concerns
the problem   each of these words
(the apricots, for one, could care less   (transmission,
meaning,
the jars remain   speechless: etc.)."   J. Derrida
                                         trans. Alan Bass
                                         "Signature Event
Context"

                                         1977, 1982)

PART TWO: THEY THOUGHT THEY LOVED ONE ANOTHER

And I have asked, have had to
Am I getting through?

Would they be writing these things
to one another
if they knew
how quickly
things can heat up
how little time there is
in which
to say?

Intimacy derives from the in   verse
of human law, and there is no law
to dictate its corruption:

       "Currently, corruption is a phenomenon that transcends
       national borders. Because new, more sophisticated
       and elaborate forms of corruption have arisen, aside
       from the classic forms, determining its causes and
       effects, as well as establishing the adequate measures
       for its prevention and sanction, has become a focal
       point in many parts of the world . . .

       The Sixth Annual Anticorruption Conference
       will be held
       in Cancún, México
       on November 22 - 25, 1993."

Some folks have a way, succinct
cannot be contradicted:

HH

I would not trust them
with my life
I would not, could not
with my life.

And why must I keep coming back
to him
or her, perhaps
that place
haunting speakeasy
not a desert at all
but green as her eyes
as one could care
them to be
under a tree
in the cool sunlight
of a May morning
someplace
in the United Kingdom
or El Paso:

Were her eyes green
Was that her touch
her 't', a tree
that flickering across my screen
could it be
we had given up
too much
to be so close?

Our times, our distances, our perceptions
our solitudes
were dissimilar
whatever the common basis
for presumed misunderstanding
fingerprints, say, as these relate to

a being fingered:

    to be caught

                              within one's own space
                    of plays, penetrations, perfumes
              fucked or caressed, even by one's own
    hand
those diverse pleasures of autonomy
                          w/o need, w/o endeavor
of which grown women and men
        know
    is not enough, no, never
was:
                    Out there here
            is space and time enough
for more space to develop, establish
longings, again, and no
con   versions need be converted, finally, erased
my old friend, of no more than two
or three
months, a forever, you who know
who and want to know
only how to hear
what might not ever, let us say
never-ever
be said:

To be a correspondent
might bring legal complications
but I'll tell you all all any   way
'piss up against that public wall' intricately, in abstract
incognito grown incontinent
listen, please
promise
not to tell . . .
closer:

PART THREE: A HISTORY MADE ONLY TO BE VIOLATED

To begin with no naive assertion
and with a thing genuine
as cigarette-smoked romance
or "you're a good man, sister"
they began by opening their hearts
and asking if all was of necessity
too mystical
too spiritual
too presenced
too new: It was.

The argument proceeded thus: that after having decided to
communicate
in the presence of others
we had no reason to be astonished
that our neighborhood would become
impoverished with invention
or prevarication, excess
or want
the apparent presence of others like and unlike
us. Why we couldn't see
through the individualistic technoid/ethnoid cant
pigmentation, no. & size of limbs, religious affiliation erotic or
a pasty Überleim predisposition favoritecerealhair cutbaud
rateclockspeedRAM
and on to the constructedness of our problem—
access of the many to significant cultural alternatives—
given the particular, shared, obscure genealogical undercurrents
bringing us together, hook or crook
in the singular brutality of the desperate fact
and despite our institutional selves (and in this wee bit of
interaction
might we easily have expected our differences
to have gone unvoiced
only for a while)—
was that not something not to be written out, ex post facto
in that medium

KK

in this age
hardly one of in   subordination?

In any case, that story obviously
has a happy ending of sorts, choice choices:
we each cling to our agencies, solitary
motivations, we tell ourselves
like a ripe peach
on a dog day, yeah—to a one
each one thinks that we're such
peaches:

But that doesn't mean
that we'll stick with it in the face of, interfaced
through thick and thin . . . "Without teeth," the interview
read, "you can't land
a minimum wage job" . . .

And the other story
the one about how superficial we'd become
in our public discourses
how unused
to conflict how sad, how sadly
private & immaterial
our politics, our working theories
could be

that one constitutes
the day.   But motion, the mind
is not simply matter.   We need both, mind you
and I—I'm still crying in my beer, and a few odd fellows, women
men faceless
though no strangers
nor to pain, with a little help, a few words
help me hang
in: [Sample follows, authored w/accomplice.]

To: ANON-L
From: jamato@ux1.cso.uiuc.edu (Joe Amato)
Subject: Re: My Recent Overview of Sunday's *MTV Unplugged*
Etc...
Cc:
Bcc:
X-Attachments:

trafficking in lingo
unplugged to mean
plugged into wirelessly
wired into sky
sky to earth
into earth unplugged
& plugged into
us into nerve
fibers of guts, pins
exposes posted outward, or knows
again from mtv
to tnc to
mbu, mebbe, to abc
of cultured anarchy   xstatic ($\geq$ 50% RH)?
carefully controlled taste?
& to match individual sensibilities:

but here's a glitch
the post posts to
strangers among us, them
us no longer we
know not what it
means to 'post' the
mtv event
or its interpretation
to all
when & where even
muddied but i do
take it to you
live from me &
just killed (as in 'you slay me') you rec'd
same to post me
back individually & not
the list & i
responding in kind write

it seems to me this activity represents the endless circulation of
public to private knowledge, & what can this be but an act of
endlessly imperfect conversion, trade?

MM

it cannot cohere unless it make money.

mtv makes money, my dears, i don't (print etc). i just write
because it pleases me, vine-ripening, & mebbe you.

let's negotiate, shall we?

first, there are a few questions i would like each of you to answer
that will help in establishing yr user profiles:

are you animal or vegetable or mineral?
male or female or hybrid?
married or single or communal?
how old are you?
what are yr ethnicities?
what is/are yr sexual orientation(s)?
are you physically or mentally dis/abled?
do you have a snmail address? what is it?
what sort of toothpaste do you buy?
with what sort of platform are you most comfortable?
do you worship at a church of yr choice?
what is yr favorite major metropolitan area, if any?

————————————————————CUT TO REDEEM————————————————————--

& as to our earlier exchange re the pain of proximity
recall that, prior to leaving, melissa
in growing discomfort
added

>and btw, i must tell you all, i'm not certain why, but i simply
must: i was
>abused as a child. my step-father beat me. you see, he would
have been a real
>man. i recall loving him...

nor is privacy the issue, for we
have chosen thus...

is it that we boyz feel safer t/here   filtered from our own active
presences   projected out into suspended likenesses metabolized
across widespread widescreen reception self-consumed in pastime
lettered in impartial anonymity milky density of territory thought
thought inprojected retinally in which what is   seen   & heard
& why seen at all? future sons (et lumiere?) of felt (father) time
synchronized as a pulse   as the throb of   words urban
eared   smelling of the street & the suburb but a rural presence too
this mustering of time to time zone through the invocation of

cybernetic (e.g.) adjectives verbalized to recombine in the
adaptive confines of a feedforward field of sodbusters   a
melting blot of consciousness a   wet dream once deferred & now
re animated   manifest if anything at all could   be & we as
able to pass ourselves off as capable in such terms   our
imprimatur to be able to begin   & end things ever so
quickly
BUT bloodless brothahs BUT & sistahs   is a gendering
if only   in retro   & some   many
most   fearing the remote   mode   (interfection)
of our requisitions   cons   piracies   of
the marketplace   s'   e   strange   ment   s?

to be revealed may not be
confession, is alive, life
speaks to, announces
the intricacies of cell, stress
of can make a body come, give
& this may be what happened: there
could be no other, or further
testing of each moment's hardship
for a reasonable fee or no
to end up bailing out, to survive

[pause to consume a pound or so of a favorite poor man's meal, macaroni
& cannellini beans... i'll be back in a few minutes to continue...]

now,   then survive the crowds, colliding exhibitionists, a
crowd even
of home, hence to weed
out the wellspring of desire
a security code, marshalling:

she signed off
w/o words.

talk talk talk &
then some   (the air here is hot & sweet at the
moment
this silence in the wake of departures, encrypted--matt,
antifreezedry & now
melissa--the silence
of the desert
incites stillness
the night
sk ey...

only to dis connect
from so much
junk, control, cr ime, so much

has gone awry, to unplugging
to lug into, nor facsimilate
a shifting elec   to   rate

mself, my bark has grown hard enough to suffer
the consequences...

((((—& only to stick to
the real
this way
as spicer implied—but commentary?—)))

ain't goin' no place
ain't virtual...

awaiting yr heartfelt responses...

love & kisses,

tomato

PART FOUR: SCHOLARLY APPARATUS (IN A NUTSHELL)

Apollinaire, writing in "Zone" (1913; trans. Roger Shattuck):

Vous avez honte when you catch yourself saying a prayer
You ridicule yourself et comme le feu de l'Enfer ton rire pétille
Les étincelles de ton rire gild the depths of your life
It is a picture pendu dans un sombre musée
And sometimes tu vas la regarder de près

Imnsho, for "Y/you/r" & "Vous/tu/ton" insert un-nostalgically *America*
& for *America*, earthy pageant of butte & shore & dale
'recall' cf. Ferlinghetti's "strange license plates/& engines" devouring same
& there is no looking, no vista to explain the symbolic drift of {TODAY}
(I know, I've traveled some)
listen to the radio (forgetting your p's & q's for a sound bite)
America, its radio a noisy mojo of happenings
& think of Merwin's bringing himself "back from the streets that open
like long/Silent laughs"
(the personal become entirely political in such re-placement)
or Foucault's "This book first arose out of a passage of Borges, out of the
laughter that shattered, as I read the passage, all the familiar landmarks of my
thought—*our* thought, the thought that bears the stamp of our age & our
geography..." *& capital appropriations etc.*

The sounds, disc/ked, taped.glued—th   nvelopeturn dupamplifie   lipping
hardly of necessity Euclidean, though longitudinal, in strictly technical terms
a body wrap, ph/s/onic—incl. *this* work, if they wish it so—meant to be seen
& heard   laughing ourselves, a chorus   into   stitches the
sounds to serve as the s-sm-smithy of a nation's consciousness   inenarrable?
or   chthonic? a world's : (cf. Vertov's "'Laboratory of Hearing,'" c. 1916)

Steiner writes about the prevalence of LP collections (*In Bluebeard's Castle*)
the "immediate common ground" of music, "private & social" (a pop
paradox) & the corresponding, declining value of 'bookishness'
but this is more than two decades back:

There is no faith, foundational   *? ⟼ write this out*
& print has opened to a plasticity
to a morphing—more, MIDI'd, anything but voiceless—might as well be
pace McLuhan   *He'll – We ld/ed*
of distant encounters f-fo-forged
w/local aliens: *⤷ avoid inhaling / in case of emergency - eye contact*

But the line holds
or doesn't
provided we breathe, or one
we must take a stand   *⟼ Women AND men ? note yr citations throughout*
mortal sorts that we are &
will never unbecome (cf. Coolidge   "Mystery is valuable and must
be preserved"):

                                               Breathe it if you like, then, I will

at times [gasp!] & no
i.e., this ≠, cannot = whol:

In standing and falling we, a country   neo   ned & full of fiber
optics   of new b orders   interstates   inter alia sed   continental
cross-hatched & always intersecting   lite   linked   neural
w/news   all   out of proportion
might   [pettinesses   copyrights treaties aside
estblsh a soil of growth   of act ual   opportunities
of inventions   that signal   discrete   positive
not the transcendence
but the evidence
of arrival   ~~arbi~~   moti   ener soun
a new site   Am   Ame   Amer   esource cod
O America   yr precarious X   ~~er matr e bodheav~~
anew re   the places up on   which   we   the age

                                                                    nd

or   ally   fin   e   ast:asa   ltc
                        it   y
             i nsol

                                                                        vent
                                                       int   he do
                        wnp   our
                                                                 a ca r
                                                                 p
                                                                 the in beg
                                                                  inning
                                                       Iro   quoi say
                                                                    s

                                           aw   o m   ant   he sky fal
                                                                       ls f
                                                                     rom the

                                                                        brin
                                     ging de   lug e
             h   ere   n   owN Yce
                  ntral   t   hey de   ad   ly   hu   nt
                                               de   light i
                                                                        ng in
                                     to   r   t ure

                                     sixteen   5   6 in
                                     F   rench Je   suits
                                               miss   ion
                                 e r e   ct e d S aint   eM   ari e
                                                                      de
                                     Gan   nen   ta   ha

                                                                      re
                                            creat   ion
                                                            east sh
                                                            ore
                       so   uth   c it yof

                                                                      the
                                            reserv   at   ion
             no   rth on par   kway
                             10'   -9 in st

                                                                      eel r
                                            ail   way
                                                                      bri
                                            dge   Clay

T   own of   villa   geo   f

a dri-
vein
onc e
h ot   standd
og
co   unt
y
p   ark
n   or th sh ore
lar geo   aks
b   ik et able sj og gers pic nic rolp ler ath bl   ades
m   use   u m

spr   ingsbrin
e
east   sh ore
nat

ion'ss alt sour   ce
sol
ar sal   t
field s
sal   t dep   let
ed
nine   teen   00

pl   ant Proce
ss
Sol   vay
a b and   oned
w   e st sh or   e
mov ed   re
al   most

so ut hs hore
city' ss   y stem
s   torm ove r
lo ads

tr   eat   was   te ment
fa   il c ity

ump
ing dr aws e w age in
to

TT

                                        m   all
                              sout hsh ore
                                  f   orm
                                  er   gaso

                                          line
                                          stor
                    age   sit   e

                          j   un   ky
                                          ard

                    an   nu alre gat
                      ta fi   shin   g
                            to   ur
                        ney   vels
                                        le
          merc   ur
                                        y
                                      dow
                                        n

                                      sol

                                      vent
                                    lev
                                        els
                                    own   d

                                      wo
        rld wa   ters   peed   re cords et

                                      here
                                        tox
                          ich ots p   ots
                    el   ligible f orf ed
      er al sup   er
                      f und   s
                                    91   8
                                        9:

                                      NO
                                STANDING
                                    6 PM

  UU

                                                                              TO
                                                                              6 AM
                         h   ave   pul   led of
         fin   to   rut   ted   p
                                                            arking   are
                                                                                 a
     ont   hesh   ores of On   on
                                                                    d   aga a
                                                                           bod
                                                                             y
                                                                             in
       a ct ive   ha
                      z   ard
                                                                           ous s t
                                                      ill   l

                                                                             ife be
                                                            l   ow
       gr   eenbla   ck cr   ests s   l   ick
                      p   ushed   a
       gain   st   r
                                                                           ocks dead
                under   gro   wth a bro
                                                                           ken
                pal   let   foam od   or of h   and ful
                                                                           lswa
                                                                           shed pebbl
                                                        estiny   s
                                                        hells alway swi
                                                                           thin
         r

                                                                           each

                                                                           acr
       oss fro   m m
                                                                              e
       wes   tsho   r
                                                                              e
       pe   o   p   le hud   dl
                                                                              e
                                                                           tog
                                            ether tent   sun der
                str   etched o   ut
                                      a   lo ngst   ate

VV

m   id   fair
                                                                w
                                                               ay
                                                               wa
                                                            iting
                                                               Pe

o   pl eof t
        he Lo   ng   ho   use
                                                           wait
                                                            ing

ww

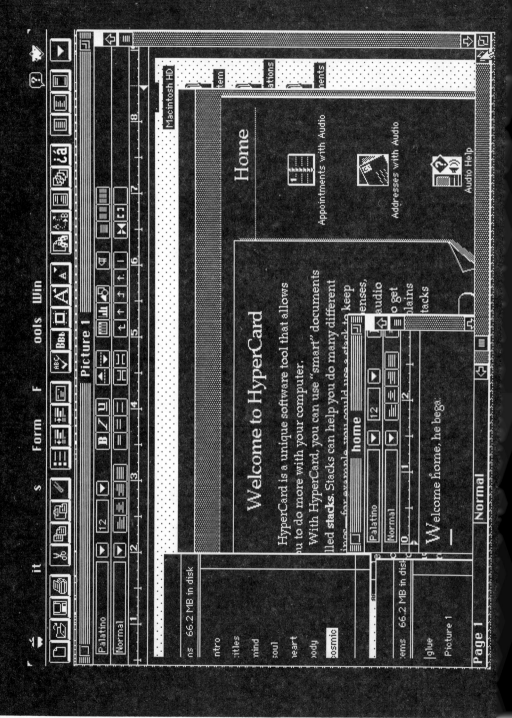